# MONEY ON THE TABLE

By

Gary Fagg
John S. Mailho

Automobile Dealer
Aftermarket Compensation

# MONEY ON THE TABLE

By

Gary Fagg
John S. Mailho

Automobile Dealer
Aftermarket Compensation

Publisher:
CREDITRE CORPORATION
4201 Brown Trail, Suite 102
Colleyville, Texas 76034
Phone: 817-788-8121
Fax: 817-788-8123



First Printing, November, 1992
Second Printing, May, 1996



---

**Library of Congress Cataloging-in-Publication Data**

Mailho, John S., 1945-
Money on the Table

Includes index
1. Insurance, Credit life-United States.
2. Insurance, Credit disability-United States
I. Fagg, Gary, 1948- II. Title
HG9977.F34 1992 368.3'2
ISBN 0-9627820-2-5

# TABLE OF CONTENTS

# Chapter One
# Introduction

Income from the sale of credit insurance and service contracts is critical to the financial success of an automobile dealership. Significant time and effort are expended on the recruitment and training of people to present these products to the customer. Systems are in place to measure the penetration of sales, but little is written to assist the dealer in maximizing the income generated by the sale of these products.

This book describes and analyzes the various forms of compensation available in the marketplace today. In selecting a method of compensation, a dealer must choose from an array of schemes—some simple and straightforward; others complex. Often, the presenter is interested in promoting a favorite scheme. The purpose of this book is to provide a clear explanation of each method in an objective manner.

Simply understanding the various methods may provide a dealer with the answer as to the best method for his dealership, but this book goes further. It compares the different methods and provides some guidance in the decision process. Still, the final decision must rest with the dealer and his insurance provider. Each dealer must consider the trade-offs between immediate cash versus deferred income, guaranteed income versus risk, and simplicity versus more complicated arrangements. Each dealership has different needs, goals and desires. Solid knowledge of the alternatives will move the dealership closer to achieving its objectives.

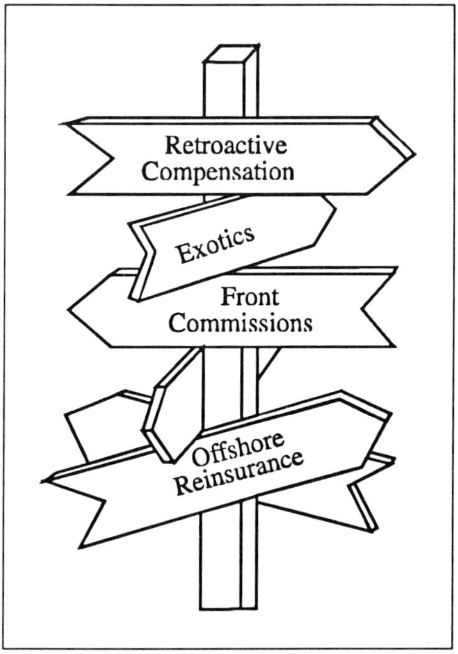


The initial discussion centers around credit life and disability insurance. Credit insurance products for dealerships remain straightforward. The standard life insurance product insuring the full gross indebtedness is pervasive where permitted. Disability insurance on the 14-day retroactive plan or the 7-day retroactive plan is almost universal. The products were once some of the simplest forms of insurance, but the complexity of policy forms, rates and procedures has increased over time. While complications have arisen because of longer term loans, the need for underwriting, and restrictive state regulations, the same products are sold today as were sold thirty years ago.

The methods to compensate the dealership, however, have evolved from simple to downright intricate. It all began with the simple proposition to pay the dealership a flat percentage of the premium collected—a **front commission**. This guaranteed compensation provided the incentive to sell the products. With compensation directly related to production, the dealership naturally had less concern about the quality of business.

In an effort to improve the quality of business, insurers began to offer **retroactive compensation**. In simplest terms, the insurer agreed to periodically evaluate the profitability of the business sold by the dealership and to share part of the profits with the dealership. Some programs were nothing more than vague promises or contained provisions that made additional compensation unlikely. Other programs were based on solid contractual and accounting provisions and provided the opportunity for real incentive compensation.

Sound retroactive compensation programs require a dealership to produce a good level of annual production, generally $50,000 or more of premium per year (although smaller dealerships may participate in pooled arrangements). Retroactive compensation can be called **one-sided reinsurance**. The dealer can earn additional income but cannot lose anything.

For large producers of premium, insurers began to offer reinsurance programs in the 1960s and 1970s. True reinsurance means risk taking; adverse claim experience reduces total income.

The early reinsurance programs were based on the formation of an Arizona reinsurance company. This was a corporation formed by the dealer that was licensed as a life insurance (or reinsurance) company. It is called a **producer-owned reinsurance company**, since all of its business is produced by the dealership. There are three drawbacks to Arizona reinsurance companies:

- The dealer must invest capital—currently $150,000.
- Only life and disability products can be reinsured (as opposed to service contracts, which are casualty insurance products).
- The reinsurer is a U.S. insurance company and subject to the extensive regulation and accounting requirements of all U.S. insurance companies.

Still, there are advantages. Formation and operation offer the dealer the opportunity to earn **underwriting profits** (premiums less expenses, reserves and claims) and **investment income** on the cash flow. Relative to insurance companies in general, producer-owned reinsurance companies are small in size. Life insurance companies, and particularly small life insurance companies, have always enjoyed favorable treatment under federal tax laws as compared to general corporations. Some insurers have developed procedures and programs that mitigate the disadvantages.

The number of single-owner Arizona reinsurers grew, but they were suitable only for the largest dealerships—those producing $250,000 or more of annual premium. For a while, smaller dealers formed reinsurance companies called **exotics**. A group of dealers banded together to form an Arizona reinsurer, enabling the capital requirements to be spread among the participants. Problems arose, however. Bickering occasionally erupted among the owners who were also competitors. Financial problems resulted when a dealer went out of business or wanted out of the arrangement.

The exotic concept grew somewhat as direct writers began to sponsor programs. The direct writer formed the reinsurance company and sold shares to the individual dealers. For an investment of about $1,000, a dealer purchased a class of stock. The underwriting profits from the dealer's business were credited directly to his class of stock along with allocated investment income. Most direct writers who were active in the automobile dealer market made this option available.

The real drive for reinsurance began in the late 1970s with the formation of **single-owner offshore reinsurance companies**. Again, the original structure was difficult. Sites like Bermuda and the Cayman Islands required substantial capital—actually more than Arizona—but there were advantages. First, an insurance company, rather than a *life* insurance company, could be formed. This permitted the reinsurance of casualty products, along with the credit life and disability insurance programs.

Second, the offshore sites offered a more reasonable regulatory climate. The United States has developed an extensive state regulatory environment for insurance companies. The primary thrust is to protect the policyholders. Most of this structure is redundant for a producer-owned reinsurer. The policyholders are protected by the regulation of the **direct writer**, the insurer whose name is on the policy. Producer-owned reinsurers only need the regulation associated with a general corporation. Other Caribbean sites were researched and developed. The favored site became the Turks and Caicos Islands, and later, the island of Nevis. The laws of the islands have evolved such that all three disadvantages of an Arizona reinsurance program were overcome. An insurance company can be formed with relatively small capitalization; can reinsure life, disability, and service contracts; and can be subject to reasonable regulation. Other Caribbean islands present similar environments and are occasionally used.

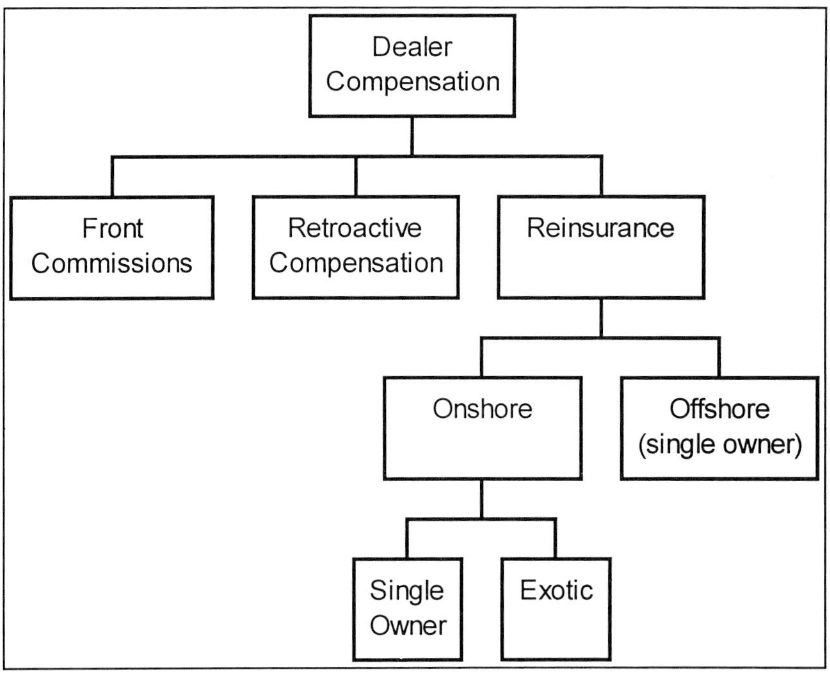

In addition to credit insurance, dealers sell service contracts or mechanical breakdown insurance; most use service contracts. A **service contract** is an indirect agreement between the customer and the insurance company with the dealership as a conduit. It provides repair coverage that wraps around and "extends" the factory warranty provided with each new car. It will also serve to extend the warranty on used cars. In general, any covered repair or service must be done at the dealership, but provisions for emergency repairs are included.

Insurers sell a casualty insurance policy to cover all the service contracts sold by the dealership. This contractual relationship is between the dealership and the insurer on behalf of the consumer. The dealership remits a specified dollar amount per car to the insurer. The charge varies by whether the car is new or used, the extent of the covered parts and services, years of coverage, and other factors. Dealerships mark up the cost to the consumer generally without restrictions; however, there are suggested retail charges supplied in the procedure manual given to the dealership. The difference between the cost to the consumer and the insurer charge is comparable to a front commission on credit life and disability products.

Additional compensation may be available from premiums remitted to the insurer. A large dealership may be offered a retroactive compensation package if the loss experience is favorable. Some dealers in offshore reinsurance programs reinsure the service contracts sold at the dealerships.

**Mechanical breakdown insurance** is required in several states. The consumer receives the same coverage as provided by service contracts, but a casualty insurance company issues an insurance policy directly to the consumer rather than indirectly through the dealership. Rates and policy forms must be filed and approved. All three compensation alternatives apply to mechanical breakdown coverage.

## Summary

All three methods of compensation—front commission, retroactive compensation and reinsurance—are viable alternatives for most dealerships. Now the problem is selecting the method appropriate for the particular dealership and structuring the corporate relationships on a sound basis to maximize income.

It's not an easy task, as the size of this book demonstrates. Understanding the nuances of the insurance products and compensation methods requires an effort—but the payoff is substantial. The opportunity for increased earnings is dramatic and, combined with the tax advantages, makes the investment in reading this book well worth the effort. After all, what you don't know leaves **MONEY ON THE TABLE**.

# Chapter Two
# Credit Life and Disability Insurance

This section presents the basics of credit life and disability products, concentrating on the aspects which directly relate to compensation or reinsurance. It is not a comprehensive treatment. The topics covered presume some familiarity with and understanding of the products.

## INSTALLMENT LOANS

Since credit insurance is tied to a specific loan, it is necessary to understand the basic structure of automobile loans that defines the insurance protection. The primary structure is **installment** or **closed-end loans**.

Installment loans are called closed-end loans because the amount and term of the loan are fixed at the inception of the loan. Most loans are repayable in equal monthly payments. The **principal** of the loan is the portion of the automobile's cost which is financed. A single premium is charged for the credit insurance. The **total amount advanced** includes the principal plus the insurance premium. Another term for the total amount advanced is the **initial net indebtedness**. At the loan's inception, the

**initial gross indebtedness** is also calculated. The scheduled interest charges over the term of the loan are determined. The initial gross indebtedness is the initial net indebtedness plus the scheduled interest charges.

Since the loan is repayable in equal monthly installments, the **monthly payment** is equal to the initial gross indebtedness divided by the term of the loan. Each monthly payment provides for the payment of the interest charges for the current month based on the remaining net indebtedness at the beginning of the month. The remainder of the monthly payment is applied to reduce the net indebtedness. The **outstanding balance** of the loan at any time is the remaining net indebtedness.

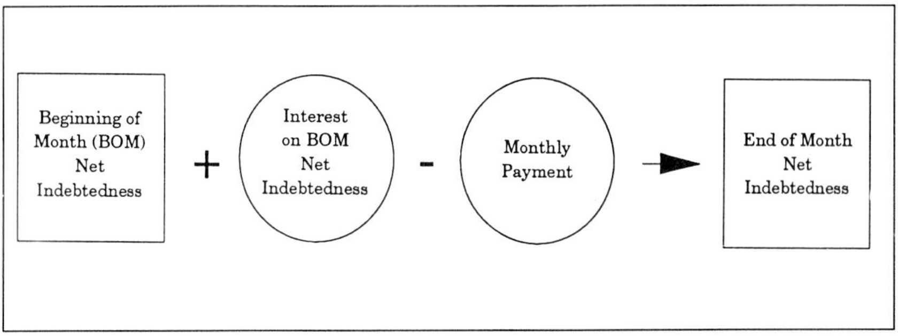


The gross indebtedness declines in equal amounts on a monthly basis. The amount of monthly decrease is equal to the loan's monthly payment. The net indebtedness declines each month also, but the pattern of the decrease is not uniform, since interest charges consume more of the early payments. Most automobile loans are for 48 or 60 months, but the following example uses a 12-month loan for simplicity.

Details of loan: 12-month term with an 18% annual interest rate compounded monthly

| | | |
|---|---|---|
| Cash advanced | $542.38 | |
| Insurance premium | 3.00 | |
| Initial net indebtedness | | $545.38 |
| Finance charges | | 54.62 |
| Total of payments (Initial gross indebtedness) | | $600.00 |

Monthly payment = $600/12 = $50

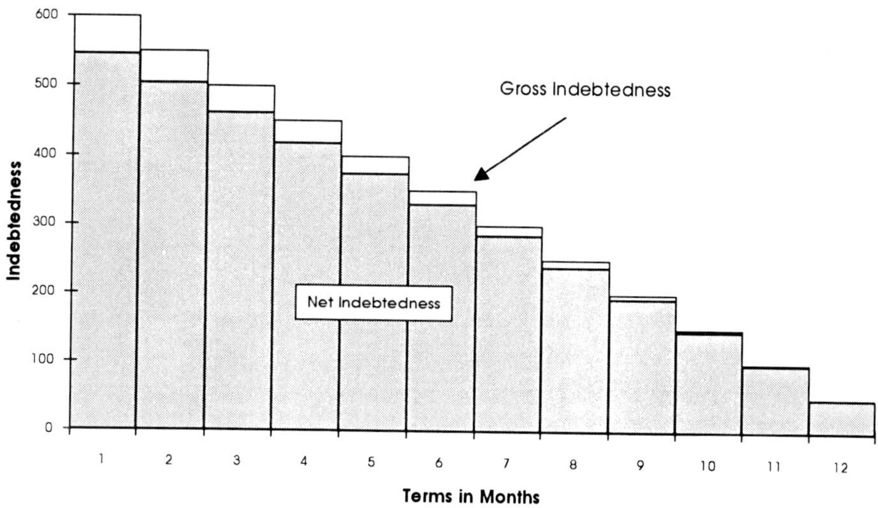


Figure 2.1. Comparison of net and gross indebtedness

| End of Month | Outstanding Net Indebtedness | Portion of Monthly Payment Applied | | Outstanding Gross Indebtedness |
|---|---|---|---|---|
| | | For Interest | To Net Indebtedness | |
| Inception | $545.38 | | | $600.00 |
| 1 | 503.56 | 8.18 | 41.82 | 550.00 |
| 2 | 461.11 | 7.55 | 42.45 | 500.00 |
| 3 | 418.03 | 6.92 | 43.08 | 450.00 |
| 4 | 374.30 | 6.27 | 43.73 | 400.00 |
| 5 | 329.91 | 5.61 | 44.39 | 350.00 |
| 6 | 284.86 | 4.95 | 45.05 | 300.00 |
| 7 | 239.13 | 4.27 | 45.73 | 250.00 |
| 8 | 192.72 | 3.59 | 46.41 | 200.00 |
| 9 | 145.61 | 2.89 | 47.11 | 150.00 |
| 10 | 97.79 | 2.18 | 47.82 | 100.00 |
| 11 | 49.26 | 1.47 | 48.53 | 50.00 |
| 12 | .00 | .74 | 49.26 | .00 |
| Total | | 54.62 | 545.38 | |

The calculations for the first monthly payment are:

Monthly interest rate = 18%/12 = **1.5%**

Portion of first payment for interest
=(beginning net indebtedness) x 1.5%
=$545.38 x .015 = **$8.18**

Portion applied to net indebtedness
= (monthly payment) - $8.18
=$50.00 - $8.18 = **$41.82**

Outstanding net indebtedness at the beginning of the second month
=(beginning net indebtedness)
- (portion applied to net indebtedness)
= $545.38 - $41.82 = **$503.56**

## CREDIT LIFE INSURANCE

One appeal of the automobile segment of the credit insurance industry is the relative uniformity of its products. The standard life products are sold virtually everywhere.

The standard product is **gross coverage uniform decreasing term insurance**, which provides life insurance protection for the full term of a monthly installment loan. The initial amount of insurance is the sum of the monthly payments—the initial gross indebtedness. Again, the gross indebtedness of the loan is the principal of the loan, the premiums for the credit insurance, plus the scheduled interest charges.

The amount of insurance decreases each month by the amount of one monthly payment. Given equal monthly payments, the result is insurance that decreases uniformly each month. If a claim occurs, the amount of insurance will exceed the loan payoff if there are no delinquencies. Proceeds go first to pay off the loan. Any remainder goes to the estate.

Gross coverage is sold wherever it is permitted. Its primary advantage is simplicity; the coverage is easily understood and explained. Rate calculations are straightforward and can even be done by hand if necessary. Even where delinquencies have occurred, the amount of insurance is usually sufficient to extinguish the debt. A final advantage is that more insurance is sold.

In several states (e.g., New York and Maine) and particular situations (e.g., loans over 60 months in Ohio and Oregon) gross coverage is not permitted. Under these circumstances, **net payoff decreasing term insurance** for the full loan term is sold. The difference is that the amount of insurance provided does **not** include the unearned interest charges. Only the net indebtedness of the loan is insured. Insurance is still decreasing term, but the pattern of decrease is not uniform from month to month.

If a claim occurs, the insurance benefit is the scheduled payoff of the loan. Most insurers pay up to two months of delinquencies. For example, if an insured dies in the eighteenth month of a three-year policy but has made only sixteen payments, the insurer will pay off the balance. But if the insured were six months delinquent, at least four delinquent payments would not be covered.

A third coverage, used in the automobile lease market, is **gross level insurance**. As the name implies, the benefit is level term insurance. This coverage is used in conjunction with one of the decreasing coverages. The decreasing coverage provides credit insurance protection for the fulfillment of the monthly lease payment, while the level coverage insures the residual value of the car that is due at the end of the lease.

For example, if the lessor died in the ninth month (having made the ninth lease payment at the beginning of the ninth month) on the policy displayed in Figure 2.2, the benefit would consist of two components. The first component is the amount of $300 to reflect the tenth, eleventh and twelfth lease payments. The second component is the level term portion covering the residual value of the lease, $400 in the example. The benefit will satisfy the entire financial obligation ($700) on the leased automobile, and the estate will own the vehicle. Newer programs, called "stream of payment" coverage, just insure the lease payments.

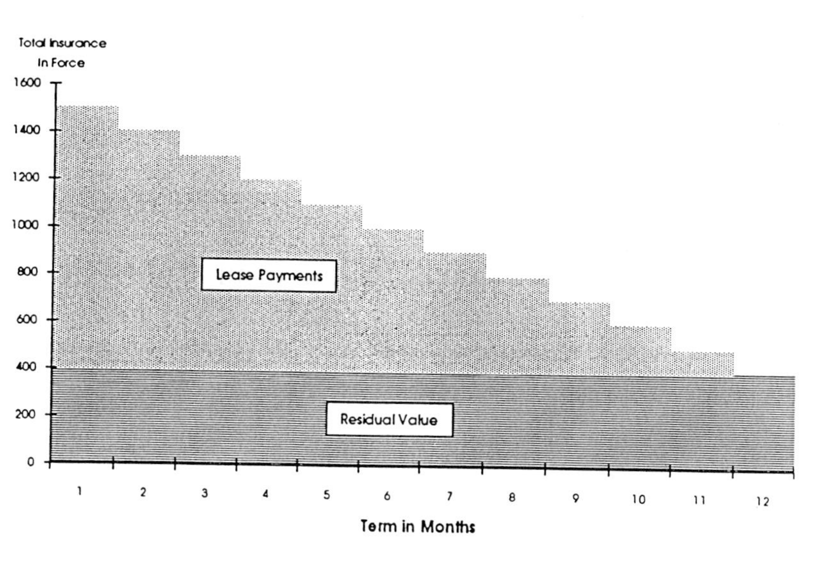


Figure 2.2. Level and decreasing coverage on leases

For all coverages, a number of provisions and options are the same. The effective date of the loan is the **effective date** of the coverage. The scheduled termination date of the loan is the **expiry date** of the insurance. All states allow **joint life coverage** when there is a co-debtor. This plan provides a death benefit if either of the co-debtors dies.

## CREDIT DISABILITY INSURANCE

The standard disability product provides for the payment of a monthly benefit equal to the loan's required monthly payment. If the insured is disabled, a payment is made once the **elimination period** is met. The elimination period is a stated number of days a claimant must remain continuously disabled before any benefits are paid. The most common coverage is **14-day retroactive coverage** (14R).

The elimination period is 14 days. If the insured remains disabled more than 14 days, a benefit is paid.

Once the elimination period has been met, the coverage may provide benefits from the first day of disability—**retroactive benefits**—or the coverage may provide benefits only for the time disabled after the elimination period—**non-retroactive benefits**.

The actual benefit is equal to one monthly payment for each completed month, plus one-thirtieth of the benefit for each additional day of disability. Under the retroactive benefit plans, an elimination period of 30 days (30R) is also available nationally, and a seven-day elimination period is available in about 20 states. Non-retroactive plans are also available for 14-day and 30-day elimination periods (14NR and 30NR).

Below are several examples of the benefits that would be provided based on different periods of disability.

| | |
|---|---|
| Coverage: | 14-day retroactive benefits |
| Days Disabled: | 60 |
| Monthly Benefit: | $300 |
| Disability Benefit | = 60 x ($300/30) |
| | = $600 |

| | |
|---|---|
| Coverage: | 14-day retroactive benefits |
| Days Disabled: | 12 |
| Monthly Benefit: | $300 |
| Disability Benefit | = 0 |

| | |
|---|---|
| Coverage: | 30-day non-retroactive benefits |
| Days Disabled: | 74 |
| Monthly Benefit: | $300 |
| | |
| Disability Benefit | = (74 - 30) x ($300/30) |
| | = $440 |

Fourteen-day retroactive coverage has proven to be the most popular coverage over time. Insureds like the short elimination period. From the dealership perspective, it is the most comprehensive product, except for seven-day retroactive coverage. Credit insurance tends to be an accept or reject decision on the part of the consumer. It makes sense to sell a more complete and higher-priced product, unless the price reaches the point where the product is rejected.

Where permitted, seven-day retroactive coverage is often sold by dealerships. With its higher cost, more consumers reject the coverage, so some dealerships still use 14-day retroactive coverage even when seven-day retroactive coverage is available. The trade-off between lower unit sales and higher dollar compensation is close. If a dealership has the option of selling a seven-day plan, it should experiment for a few months and measure the impact on sales and commission income.

There is no evidence that selling one of the lower-priced plans (14NR, 30R, or 30NR) creates enough additional sales to offset the lower dollar compensation. Customers prefer 14-day retroactive anyway. Insureds who become disabled generally need the benefit from day one and are certainly happier with the coverage.

The table below illustrates the difference in single premium rates for the various plans for a 48-month loan in Maryland:

| Plan | Single Premium per $100 of Initial Gross Indebtedness | Cost for a $10,000 Loan |
|---|---|---|
| 7-day Retro | $5.18 | $518 |
| 14-day Retro | $3.91 | $391 |
| 14-day Non-Retro | $3.18 | $318 |
| 30-day Retro | $3.45 | $345 |
| 30-day Non-Retro | $2.64 | $264 |

## Pre-existing Conditions

Credit insurance is offered without medical questions or with medical questions that relate only to serious illness. The cost of underwriting and the delays in accepting coverage are not acceptable given the size of the credit insurance premium and the amount of coverage. Still, the borrower may have existing impairments which may cause future disabilities. A **pre-existing condition** is an impairment for which the insured has been treated prior to the effective date of the insurance.

Insurers have the option of covering pre-existing conditions or excluding them. If pre-existing conditions are excluded, the standard exclusion is a **six and six**

**exclusion**. Under this exclusion, a disability is **not covered** if:

> the insured received treatment within the six months prior to the effective date of the insurance,
>
> **and**
>
> the insured is disabled due to the pre-existing condition within six months after the effective date of the insurance.

Both conditions must be met. If the last treatment precedes the effective date by more than six months, the disability is covered. If the disability starts more than six months after the effective date, the disability is covered.

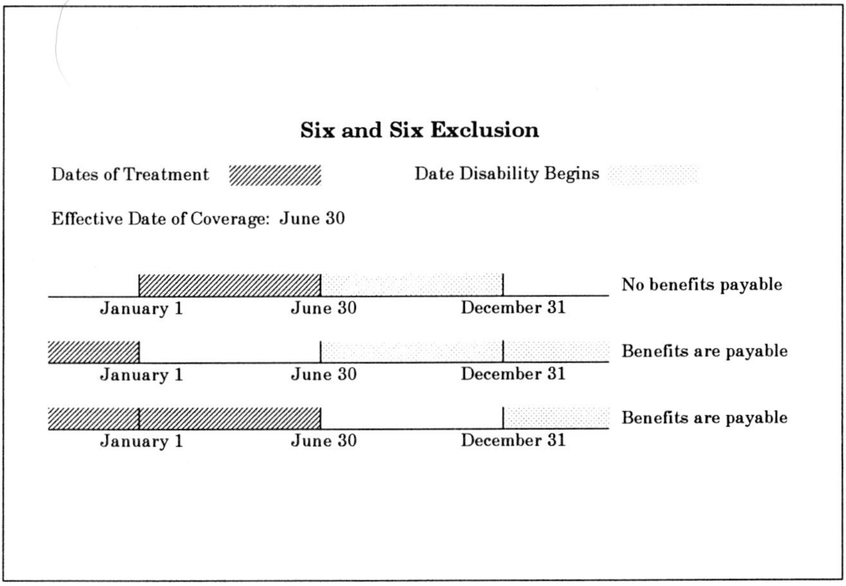

Below are examples of how the exclusion is applied.

| Effective Date of Coverage | Date of Last Treatment | Date Disability Began | Benefits Payable |
|---|---|---|---|
| 6-30-92 | 3-15-92 | 9-15-92 | No |
| 6-30-92 | 3-15-92 | 3-15-93 | Yes |
| 6-30-92 | 9-15-91 | 9-15-92 | Yes |
| 6-30-92 | 9-15-91 | 3-15-93 | Yes |

In some states, insurers are permitted to charge an additional 10% of premium if pre-existing conditions are covered. Since the decision by the consumer is an accept or reject decision, it is generally to the dealership's favor to sell a product covering pre-existing conditions. The coverage generates more dollars of compensation and higher customer satisfaction. Unfortunately, customers take advantage of the coverage and buy it with the knowledge of a likely disability claim. As a result, the 10% surcharge is often inadequate. A number of insurers no longer offer the option.

## PREMIUM STRUCTURE AND RATES

The dominant features that affect compensation are the structure of the premiums and the rates that are charged. All credit insurance sold in the automobile market segment is sold on a **single premium** basis. One premium is charged at the inception of the policy for the total coverage provided over the term of the loan. The cost of the insurance is added to the portion of the purchase price which is financed to produce the initial net indebtedness of the loan.

The up-front single premium is a clear advantage to the insurer and the dealership. The dealership receives its compensation for the sale immediately. Dealerships using a **report and remittance** procedure (see Figure 3.3) deduct compensation from the premium remittance sent to the insurer. For dealerships on the **billing method**, the applications are remitted to the insurer. Then the dealership receives a bill for the amount due the insurer which is net of the commission due the dealership.

A **premium refund** is always rebated to the borrower if the loan (and the insurance) is terminated prior to the scheduled maturity date of the loan. A portion of the single premium is then returned to the customer. This amount represents a return of the premium for the unused portion of the original risk insured. If a death claim occurs, the life insurance premium is generally considered fully earned, but there is a refund of the unearned disability premium.

On a typical group of credit insurance certificates, about 20% of the original premium will be refunded over the term of the certificates. The largest number of refunds occurs in the first month, mostly customers who change their minds about wanting the insurance ("buyer's remorse"). After that, there is a relatively steady stream of refunds. Loans are repaid because of trade-ins or involuntary termination due to accidents or repossessions. Some people just pay off their loans early.

The insurer treats the premium refund as a negative premium. The typical premium remittance form requires the calculation of **net written premiums**, also called **G-R premiums**. The premiums on the new policies issued in the month are the **gross written premiums** (G). Premium refunds (R) are deducted from the gross written premiums to produce net written premiums.

Of equal significance to the premium structure is the level of premiums. Each state has adopted a **prima facie premium rate** which is the maximum premium rate that can be charged in the state without actuarial justification for a higher rate. Insurers are permitted to charge a lower rate, but none do in the automobile market. Also, it is virtually impossible to get an **upward deviation**—a rate higher than the prima facie rate. So, practically all automobile business is sold at prima facie rates. As a sidelight, the term "prima facie" rate means a rate judged by the state "on its face" to be reasonable in relation to benefits provided to the insureds.

Credit insurance is the only form of life or disability insurance where the rates are specified in state regulations. Even so, the rates are not directly regulated. The insurance commissioner only has the right "to disapprove policies if the benefits provided are not reasonable in relation to the premium charged."

Premium rates for life insurance are expressed in the form 50¢/$100/year. In most states, this means the rate is 50¢ for each $100 of initial gross indebtedness, for each year of coverage. For example, if the initial gross indebtedness on a 48-month car loan is $10,000, the gross premium is:

$$50¢/\$100/\text{year} \times \frac{10{,}000}{100} \times \frac{48 \text{ months}}{12 \text{ months}}$$

$$= .50 \times 100 \times 4$$

$$= \$200$$

Although the premium rate is expressed per $100 of initial gross indebtedness, its derivation reflects the fact that the coverage provided is decreasing term insurance. Rates for net payoff coverage and level insurance are also expressed in cents/$100/year. These premium rates are higher to adjust for the different patterns of insurance benefits provided.

Unlike the premium rates for most life and disability insurance products, premium rates for credit insurance are not age-rated. One rate is charged for all ages (**uniage**) and both sexes (**unisex**). This means, first of all, that the products are a better buy for older people and for men. On average, women have mortality rates that are about 60% of men's. This is reflected in the rates charged for joint insurance but not for single life coverage.

Each state sets the rate for joint life insurance as a percentage of the single life rate. Multiples vary from 150% to 180%. At a 160% multiple, joint life coverage for the example on the previous page costs:

$$1.60 \times \$200 = \$320$$

The rates for disability insurance are also expressed per $100 of initial gross indebtedness. In each state regulation, a table specifies a rate for each term of insurance. A typical table for 14-day retroactive coverage is:

| Term in Months | Rate per $100 |
|---|---|
| 12 | $2.20 |
| 24 | 3.00 |
| 36 | 3.60 |
| **48** | **4.20** |
| 60 | 4.80 |

For the example above, which has a $10,000 initial gross indebtedness and a 48-month term, the disability premium to insure the primary debtor is:

$$\$4.20 \times \frac{10{,}000}{100}$$

$$= \$420$$

Joint disability insurance is rarely sold. From an actuarial standpoint, the multiple should exceed 2.00—females have higher disability rates than males. In the few states where it is permitted, the approved multiples are 160% to 200%. The cost is rather prohibitive.

A major feature of state regulation is the wide diversity of prima facie rates by state. Since the coverage must match the loan provisions, the benefits of credit insurance policies are virtually identical. The same life coverage sold in New York for 39¢/$100/year is sold in Louisiana for $1.00/$100/year. One might wonder why all the insurers are not down in the South fighting for business. The answer is that commission levels are what really vary. Commission levels are dramatically higher in Louisiana than New York.

As a broad statement, the insurers need about 30¢/$100/year to provide for claims, general operating costs, premium taxes and profit. The rest goes for compensation to the dealership and general agents. Total compensation on life insurance is about 10-15% in New York, while it is about 55-65% in Louisiana. From the insurer standpoint, the states are nearly identical. Compensation has risen over the years to the point that the insurer receives the same net dollars in the door regardless of the premium rate charged to the consumer.

Figure 2.3 shows the approximate prima facie premium rate in each state. Prima facie rates are also set for disability insurance, although the wide diversity is not as evident. Over the last thirty years, a great deal of attention has been given to the life insurance rates, but very little to the disability rates. Most states have not changed the disability rates adopted in the 1960s.

| State | Single Life | Disability 14R (48 mo.) | State | Single Life | Disability 14R (48 mo.) |
|---|---|---|---|---|---|
| Alabama | 0.80 | 4.30 | Missouri | 0.55 | 4.30 |
| Alaska | 0.49 | 2.79 | Montana | 0.60 | 4.30 |
| Arizona | 0.44 | 3.79 | Nebraska | 0.55 | 3.85 |
| Arkansas | 0.65 | 4.13 | Nevada | 0.65 | 4.30 |
| California | 0.42 | 5.05 | New Hampshire | 0.42 | 3.33 |
| Colorado | 0.52 | 3.87 | New Jersey | 0.40 | 2.49 |
| Connecticut | 0.50 | 3.32 | New Mexico | 0.65 | 4.14 |
| Delaware | 0.65 | 4.30 | New York | 0.39 | 6.06 |
| D. C. | 0.49 | (1) | North Carolina | 0.55 | 4.40 |
| Florida | 0.50 | 3.44 | North Dakota | 0.40 | 3.40 |
| Georgia | 0.45 | 4.60 | Ohio | 0.50 | 3.93 |
| Hawaii | 0.40 | 3.16 | Oklahoma | 0.68 | 4.60 |
| Idaho | 0.54 | 4.30 | Oregon | 0.42 | 4.05 |
| Illinois | 0.47 | 3.90 | Pennsylvania | 0.50 | 3.45 |
| Indiana | 0.65 | 4.15 | Rhode Island | 0.46 | 4.02 |
| Iowa | 0.47 | 3.69 | South Carolina | 0.65 | 3.40 |
| Kansas | 0.65 | 4.30 | South Dakota | 0.60 | 3.87 |
| Kentucky | 0.65 | 6.36 | Tennessee | 0.66 | 4.13 |
| Louisiana | 1.00 | 4.60 | Texas | 0.36 | 3.55 |
| Maine | 0.30 | (2) | Utah | 0.42 | 3.58 |
| Maryland | 0.56 | 3.91 | Vermont | 0.35 | 3.00 |
| Massachusetts | 0.45 | (2) | Virginia | 0.41 | 3.77 |
| Michigan | 0.48 | 4.30 | Washington | 0.60 | 4.30 |
| Minnesota | 0.40 | 3.88 | West Virginia | 0.65 | 3.65 |
| Mississippi | 0.80 | 5.40 | Wisconsin | 0.39 | 3.12 |
| | | | Wyoming | 0.50 | 4.30 |

(1) Rates are not promulgated
(2) 14R coverage is not permitted, 30NR is available

Life rates are the single premium rates per $100 initial gross indebtedness for a 12-month term.
Disability rates are per $100 initial gross indebtedness for 14R for a 48-month term.
Rates in effect January 1, 1996

Due to the complexity of prima facie rating in some states, these rates should be used only for comparison purposes.

Figure 2.3 Approximate prima facie rates by state as of January 1, 1996

# Chapter Three
# Front Commissions

## FRONT COMMISSIONS

Front commissions are guaranteed compensation for the sale of credit insurance products and are a part of all compensation programs. They are a flat percentage of net written premiums. Insurers set the percentage by state, reflecting the prima facie rate that is charged in the state and other characteristics of the business. Since the single premium is paid in one sum at issue, so are the front commissions.

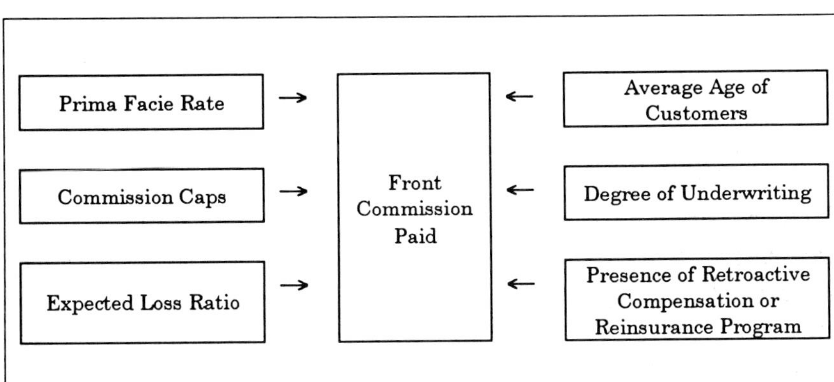


Figure 3.1. Influences on front commission level

Until the last few years, it was common practice to pay the same percentage of compensation on both the life and disability products. In the 1960s and 1970s the usual result was that the insurer made a profit on the life insurance product but lost money on the disability product. Insurers really consider the two products as one line of business. They set commission levels based on the combined net income of the two products.

### Prima Facie Rates

In setting prima facie rates, states theoretically consider the **benchmark loss ratio**. A **loss ratio** is the ratio of benefits to premiums. A benchmark loss ratio is the loss ratio that is judged by state legislators or regulators to provide a reasonable level of benefits—most states adopted 50%. In theory, the state measures the cost of benefits and divides by the benchmark loss ratio to calculate the prima facie rates. In reality, most prima facie rates are set in the political arena by negotiation rather than actuarial science.

As it turns out, actual loss ratios for life insurance are generally below the benchmarks, but loss ratios for disability insurance often exceed the benchmarks. Except in the South where prima facie rates tend to be higher, the combined loss ratios are fairly close to the benchmarks.

Two factors have caused some insurers to change their practices regarding front commission percentages. First, claim costs for life insurance have decreased continuously over the last thirty years, but disability claim costs have remained steady or even increased. Second, consumer advocates criticized the cost of life insurance without any comment about the cost of disability insurance. Although most state regulators were satisfied with a reasonable combined loss ratio, there was steady downward pressure on life rates. In many states, life rates are less than one-half the rates charged in 1960. Some relief has been provided on disability insurance. California and New York, with two of the lowest life rates, have two of the highest sets of disability rates.

Still, the loss ratios on disability insurance usually exceed the loss ratios on life insurance. To reflect this fact, insurers have begun to vary the compensation percentage on the two products. The primary rationale is that the life insurance product remains more profitable than the disability product, so it should be stressed.

Most states have rate stability. Rates are reviewed and changed every five to ten years. A number of states, however, introduce complexity into the credit insurance programs by requiring frequent periodic rate changes. The extreme example is Pennsylvania. It requires insurers to review loss ratios every year and to adjust rates *by dealership* to achieve the benchmark loss ratio. Maine, New Hampshire, New York, Vermont, and Wisconsin also require rerating every two or three years. Several other states, including Massachusetts and Ohio, require the Insurance Department to review loss experience every few years and to adjust the statewide prima facie rate. There is a clear trend for more frequent rate changes, which introduces added complexity to what was once a simple product. Every rate change forces an insurer to review (and possibly adjust) the level of front commissions.

## Commission Caps

A significant element of compensation in some states is **commission caps**. In the 1960s, there was a move to impose caps on commissions as an indirect method of controlling premium rates and protecting insurer solvency. Before the trend subsided, about half of the states adopted caps on commissions. Figure 3.2 shows the states with commission caps and the percentage imposed. These limitations have substantially affected the structure of credit insurance compensation over the years. Many of the reinsurance programs were developed as a legal mechanism to generate potential total income in excess of the commission caps.

In general, commission caps have not served a useful purpose. Enforcement has been haphazard except in a few states. Caps certainly do not have any impact on the price paid by the consumer. Most insurers, however, have at least attempted to comply with the letter of the law.

The biggest problem with the enforcement of the caps is the difficulty in wording a regulation to specify every method of providing compensation. All of the parties involved—insurers, general agents, and dealerships—have demonstrated remarkable creativity in finding loopholes in the various regulations.

In general, the regulations specify a limit on compensation, expressed as a percentage of net written premiums. Some states have a limit on total compensation; some have separate limitations on the dealership and the general agent, and some just limit the amount paid to the dealership. Although expressed as a percentage of premium, the definition of compensation often includes any form of value transferred for the sale of the insurance products. (Since insurers have traditionally provided rate calculation material or machines, these items are normally excluded.)

| State | Automobile Dealer | General Agent | Total Compensation |
|---|---|---|---|
| Arkansas | 40% | 10% | |
| California | Life - 27.50%<br>Disability - 23.75% | Life - 7.50%<br>Disability 6.25% | Life - 35%<br>Disability - 30% |
| Indiana | 35% | 7.5% | 42.5% |
| Maine | 10% | 5% | |
| Maryland | 32% | 4% | 36% |
| Mississippi | | | 45% |
| Missouri | 40% | 10% | |
| Montana | | | 40% Unofficial |
| Nebraska | 30% | | |
| Nevada | | | 40% |
| New York | Service Fee Only 5-10% | 5-6%<br>Dept. Guidelines | |
| Oklahoma | | | 40% |
| Oregon | | | 35% |
| Pennsylvania | Life - 27%<br>Disability - 21% | Life - 3%<br>Disability 4% | Life - 30%<br>Disability - 25% |
| South Dakota | | | 40% |
| Washington | 40% | | |

Figure 3.2. Commission caps by state as of January 1, 1996

Commissions paid up front and any retroactive commissions paid later are included in the calculation.

Below is a typical commission cap regulation; this one applies to Arkansas business.

**Regulation No. 12.14.1: "As to credit life or credit disability insurance written by or through a creditor, or any affiliate, associate, subsidiary, director, officer, employee or other representative of or for such creditor, or by or through any agent or broker, all compensation for writing or handling such insurance shall not exceed forty percent (40%) of the maximum premiums permitted herein."**

The primary exception is for reinsurance. Underwriting profits and investment income earned in a reinsurance company are not included in most regulations. These profits are not considered compensation, since they are not guaranteed. In theory, they are not earnings from the sale of products but, rather, a return for the assumption of the insurance risk on the business. This is proper and correct. The earnings of a reinsurer are the same as the earnings of other insurance companies. There are also some practical considerations. For instance, it is impossible to fairly test whether these earnings exceed the cap percentage. Reinsurance earnings vary from year to year based on loss experience; the results of one year may exceed the cap, while other years produce losses. No one has an administrative system that could match the reinsurance earnings with the original front compensation. In any event, it takes five or more years to determine the final reinsurance earnings.

## Expected Loss Ratio and Average Age

Another element in the compensation picture is the expected loss experience of the individual dealership. All dealerships charge the same premium rate in a state, but not all dealerships have the same expected loss ratio. This arises primarily because of the uniage rating. A typical group of credit insurance buyers will have an average age of 39. Dealerships with a lower average age of buyers will have lower expected loss ratios, and the converse is true. The average age of the dealership's clientele will be reflected in the average age of the insurance buyers. Many dealerships now sell several makes, so that their clientele provides a good mix of ages. But a Lincoln or Cadillac dealer will have a significantly higher average age. This is likely to be reflected in the front commission offered.

The average age also affects disability claim costs, but the impact is not as dramatic. Costs do rise with age, but the increase in costs is much slower than for life insurance. This pattern results from a combination of frequency and severity of claims. The probability of disability from accidents decreases with age, since younger people are more likely to have physically demanding occupations. As expected, the probability of disability from sickness increases with age. In addition, given an identical disability, a younger person will likely recover faster.

Several other factors do have an impact on the expected loss ratio. The percentage of women buyers affects the life claim cost, but this statistic is not maintained, so it is not considered.

## Underwriting

Underwriting is a significant consideration. Credit insurance is still written without any underwriting, but the trend is definitely towards underwriting. People have become more knowledgeable about the availability of credit insurance and take advantage of it. Borrowers are said to **anti-select** against the insurer when they buy insurance with the knowledge of a serious health defect. **Anti-selection** has always existed, but it has increased in the last few years—particularly relating to AIDS. One study several years ago found that 5% of all credit life claims were cancer claims with the date of death occurring within six months after the date of issue.

A simple form of underwriting is a **good health statement**. The insured just signs a statement that says he is in good health to the best of his knowledge and belief. This is a palatable form of underwriting, since it does not detract from the sale. However, it provides the insurer with only a limited defense at claim time.

The usual underwriting is based on one to three questions concerning whether the insured has or has not been treated for a list of specified terminal diseases. Where permitted, this list includes AIDS. This form clearly interrupts the sale of products, but the impact on claims is material. While definitive studies have not been done, it is estimated that underwriting will reduce claims by 5%-10%, sometimes more. Underwriting is not pleasant, but it is likely to be necessary in the future if current commission levels are to be maintained.

## Other Compensation

In general, a compensation program that involves only front commission will pay the highest front commission. When the total program involves the potential for additional earnings through retroactive compensation or reinsurance, the insurer will usually require a lower front commission. The dealership must forgo some guaranteed front money for the potential that total earnings will ultimately exceed the amount the insurer will guarantee.

## REFUNDS AND RETURN COMMISSIONS

The compensation paid up front is a percentage of net written premiums. This percentage is negotiated between the insurer (or the general agent) and the dealership. Positive compensation is produced by applying the percentage to the gross premiums, but the dealership must pay back the unearned commissions on premium refunds. This is called a **chargeback of commission** on refund or **return commissions**. Figure 3.3 is a typical report and remittance form showing how the actual commissions are determined.

Each new sale produces new commission income, but a refund is a negative sale. For the most part, the dealership is powerless to combat refunds. Insureds are not under any obligation to keep the insurance in force. After the first few months that a policy is in force, refunds are primarily caused by a termination of the loan through a trade-in, loan prepayment, or repossession.

REPORT AND REMITTANCE
SOUND AND PROFITABLE LIFE INSURANCE COMPANY

Account Name________________ Group Policy #________

Individual completing this report______________ Date_____

Total number of certificates/cancellations________

| | Credit Life | Credit Dis. |
|---|---|---|
| A. Premium Charged This Month | $______ | $______ |
| B. Premium Refunded This Month | -(______) | -(______) |
| C. Total (A-B) | $______ | $______ |
| D. Commission Rate | X______% | X______% |
| E. Subtotal Commissions (CxD) | $______ | $______ |
| F. Total Remittance (C-E) | $______ | $______ |
| G. Grand Total | | $______ |

Check #________ enclosed for $________

Figure 3.3. Typical report and remittance form

The majority of refunds in the first few months are insureds who just have a change of heart. It is important that the dealership treat these customers as a new sale. This is difficult—the sale is over, and the opportunity to retain the insured usually must be made over the phone. Mostly, the insured just needs reassurance that the initial decision to purchase the product was sound.

The objections will be the same as those faced on the initial sale. The key is to direct the call to the F&I person trained to respond to these objections. The receptionist or salesperson must hand the insured off to the F&I person—otherwise the credit insurance sale will probably be lost. The dealership should formalize this procedure so that all personnel who are in contact with customers know to turn over the customer to the F&I desk. If not, the dealership will leave **MONEY ON THE TABLE**.

## Methods to Earn Commissions

A major element in the financial statements of the dealership is whether to establish a liability for future return commissions. Most dealerships do not establish the liability, since the liability is usually not deductible for tax purposes. To accurately reflect net income, some provision should be made for future return commissions.

The method used to account for commission income has a material effect on the dealership's net income. There are three ways to reflect commission income in the financials:

- Take commissions on new sales less return commissions directly into income (cash basis).

- Take commission income on new sales into income, but hold a liability for future refunds on past sales.

- Take commissions into income on an earned basis by holding a liability for unearned commissions.

Certainly the first option is the most prevalent, but the financially prudent dealership of today will recognize that a future liability exists. Commissions taken into income in past accounting periods will produce negative income in the future. This is not a problem when sales are good, but it worsens the results when sales are down.

To establish a liability for methods two and three, it is necessary to calculate the unearned commissions. One method is to have the insurer periodically provide the dealership with the amount of **unearned gross premiums** on its business. Unearned premiums are the portion of the original single premiums representing the value of the unexpired insurance. The unearned commissions are simply the front commission percentage times the unearned premiums.

A decision must now be made whether to use method two or three. The logic of method two is that the front commission is for the sale. Since the sale is complete, the money can be taken into income, but a provision is made for the "negative sales" (refunds) that will occur in the future. At any point in time, about 15%-20% of the existing unearned premiums will be refunded in the future. Let's use 20%. The return commission liability equals:

.20 x (front commission percentage) x
(unearned premiums)

This is the estimate of the return commissions the dealership must pay back to the insurer in the future based on the policies already sold.

The most conservative accounting treatment is to earn the commission over the term of the insurance contract. Although this is the slowest method for earning commissions, it automatically and accurately provides for future return commissions.

**Credit Life Insurance**
**Refund and Commission Patterns**
**Based on 48-Month Term Business - One Month of Production**

| End of Policy Month | Percentage of Total Refunds Paid in Month % | Cash Premiums (Refunds) in Month $ | **Method 1** Cash Commissions in Month (40%) $ | Liability for Future Return Commissions $ | **Method 2** Commission Taken into Income $ | Unearned Commission $ | **Method 3** Earned Commission in Month $ |
|---|---|---|---|---|---|---|---|
| Issue | -0- | 10,000 | 4,000 | (680) | 3,320 | 4,000 | -0- |
| 1 | 6.6 | (112) | (45) | (635) | 0 | 3,837 | 118 |
| 2 | 4.2 | (71) | (28) | (607) | 0 | 3,677 | 132 |
| 3 | 3.4 | (57) | (23) | (584) | 0 | 3,521 | 133 |
| 4 | 3.4 | (57) | (23) | (561) | 0 | 3,368 | 130 |
| 5 | 3.3 | (56) | (22) | (539) | 0 | 3,218 | 128 |
| 6 | 3.2 | (54) | (22) | (517) | 0 | 3,072 | 124 |
| 7 | 3.5 | (59) | (24) | (493) | 0 | 2,929 | 119 |
| 8 | 3.9 | (66) | (26) | (467) | 0 | 2,790 | 113 |
| 9 | 3.6 | (61) | (24) | (443) | 0 | 2,654 | 112 |
| 10 | 3.7 | (63) | (25) | (418) | 0 | 2,521 | 108 |
| 11 | 3.8 | (64) | (26) | (392) | 0 | 2,392 | 103 |
| 12 | 3.5 | (59) | (24) | (368) | 0 | 2,266 | 102 |
| 13 | 4.1 | (69) | (28) | (340) | 0 | 2,144 | 94 |
| 14 | 3.6 | (61) | (24) | (316) | 0 | 2,025 | 95 |
| 15 | 3.5 | (59) | (24) | (292) | 0 | 1,909 | 92 |
| 16 | 3.4 | (57) | (23) | (269) | 0 | 1,797 | 89 |
| 37 | 0.5 | (8) | (3) | (10) | 0 | 225 | 38 |
| 38 | 0.4 | (7) | (3) | (7) | 0 | 188 | 34 |
| 39 | 0.3 | (5) | (2) | (5) | 0 | 154 | 32 |
| 40 | 0.2 | (3) | (1) | (4) | 0 | 123 | 30 |
| 41 | 0.2 | (3) | (1) | (3) | 0 | 96 | 26 |
| 42 | 0.1 | (2) | (1) | (2) | 0 | 72 | 23 |
| 43 | 0.1 | (2) | (1) | (1) | 0 | 51 | 20 |
| 44 | 0.1 | (2) | (1) | 0 | 0 | 34 | 16 |
| 45 | 0.0 | 0 | 0 | 0 | 0 | 20 | 14 |
| 46 | 0.0 | 0 | 0 | 0 | 0 | 10 | 10 |
| 47 | 0.0 | 0 | 0 | 0 | 0 | 3 | 7 |
| 48 | 0.0 | 0 | 0 | 0 | 0 | 0 | 3 |
| Totals | 100.0 | | 3,320 | | 3,320 | | 3,320 |
| Net Written Premium | | 8,310 | | | | | |
| Refunds | | (1,690) | | | | | |

Figure 3.4. Methods to earn commissions

Earned Commissions for the Month =
(Premiums and refunds in the month) x
(commission percentage)
\+ Unearned commissions at the beginning of the month
\- Unearned commissions at the end of the month

## Walkaway Commissions

There is an occasional practice called **walkaway commissions**. Here the dealership is not responsible for return commissions. If an insured cancels his policy after a specified period following issue (e.g., 90 days), the dealership is relieved from paying back return commissions. The practice is fairly common in Canada, but it is unusual in the United States.

It sounds wonderful at first, but it is generally not a benefit to the dealership. The lack of chargeback represents a cost to the insurer, so the insurer will reduce front commissions. This cost is estimated by the insurer and converted to a percentage of original written premium. Then, the level of front commissions is reduced. The insurer is usually conservative in its estimate of the refunds that will occur, so the reduction in the front commissions more than offsets the chargebacks that will occur. This is similar to dealership calculations of residual value on walkaway leases—the expected value in the future will be conservatively discounted. In addition, the reduction in front commission occurs when the policy is sold, while the return commissions occur during the policy term. This is a time value of money argument that cannot be ignored. The reduced cash up front costs the dealership lost investment income for use of the cash.

The following percentages are the approximate front commission percentages an insurer will pay based on various chargeback periods, given a 40% commission if commissions are always charged back. Most walkaway programs have a requirement that commissions be returned for at least a minimum period of time following policy issue—30, 60, or 90 days.

At a 40% front commission, the equivalent walkaway commission is:

| Period after Issue Commissions Must Be Returned | Equivalent Commission Percentage |
|---|---|
| never | 30% |
| 30 days | 32% |
| 60 days | 33% |
| 90 days | 34% |
| always | 40% |

# Chapter Four
# Retroactive Compensation

## RETROACTIVE COMPENSATION

In an effort to attract more business, and to attract better quality business, insurers may offer **retroactive compensation**, commonly called **retros**. A retro is a promise by the insurer to share part of the underwriting profit with the dealership. Periodically, the loss experience of the dealership's business is calculated, and the profits are determined. A percentage of these profits is paid to the dealership in addition to the front commission, so long as the total compensation does not exceed the commission cap in the state. Retros have been called **one-sided reinsurance**. The dealership can earn additional income, but it does not have any liability if the loss experience is not favorable. The retro cannot be less than zero. An automobile dealership is not an insurance company, so it cannot undertake insurance liabilities.

## THE RETRO AGREEMENT

The promise to pay a retro is usually contained in a written document. It may be incorporated into the group policy issued to the dealership, in the agent's agreement with the dealership, or simply in a letter signed by an officer of the insurer. When a general agent is involved, the document may be between the general agent and the dealership. The important consideration is that the promise be made in writing and executed by an officer of the company with the authority to extend the offer.

The document will contain three important elements:

- the formula for the calculation, including the portion deducted by the insurer for administration and risk,

- the timing of the payments, and

- the termination provision.

Figure 4.1 shows a sample retro agreement.

The agreement will specify the percentage of the profit that is shared with the dealership. The percentage may be 100%. In this case, the insurer retains its administrative fee and earns investment income, but all of the underwriting profit is returned to the dealership. For smaller dealerships, the insurer may share only part of the profit.

The percentage shared usually depends on the level of annual production. A sample scale is as follows:

| Annual Production | Percentage of Profit Received by Dealership |
|---|---|
| $ 0 - $50,000 | None |
| $ 50,001 - $100,000 | 25% |
| $100,001 - $125,000 | 50% |
| $125,001 - $150,000 | 75% |
| $150,001 and over | 100% |

An alternative is for the insurer or general agent to offer a pooled retro. The insurer may agree to combine the experience of all automobile dealers in the state whose annual production is less than $50,000. Then the profits of the pool are divided based on the earned premium of each dealership. The allocation may be made for just the profitable accounts, but some insurers pay each dealership regardless of individual experience.

The logic of paying both good and bad accounts in a pool is that, for small accounts, the difference between profit and loss may be one claim. For a group of twenty-five $10,000 accounts, the approximate number of expected claims in a year is only ten. The ten accounts where the claims occur will be unprofitable, while all the others are profitable. Over a number of years, the claims will likely be spread among all the dealerships. This combining of small groups to spread the risk is one role of an insurance company.

## THE RETRO FORMULA

The retro formula is generally on an **inception-to-date (ITD)** basis. For a particular dealership, each element in the formula represents the total of all amounts since the dealership began doing business with the insurer. If the dealership first wrote business on January 1, 1990, this date is the **inception date**. Typically,

## RETROACTIVE COMPENSATION ADDENDUM

This Addendum effective as of ___________ is attached to and by reference incorporated into that certain Agency Agreement dated _______ between _____________________________ (hereinafter referred to as "Company") and _____________________________ (hereinafter referred to as "Agent").

NOW THEREFORE, IT IS MUTUALLY UNDERSTOOD AND AGREED AS FOLLOWS:

I. **RETROACTIVE COMPENSATION**

In addition to any compensation provided for in said Agency Agreements and Schedules attached thereto:

A. As of ___________ and each __________ thereafter prior to the termination of this Agreement, the Company shall render an accounting to the Agent reflecting the experience on policies and/or certificates written by the Agent as follows:

1. _________ percent (____%) of the inception-to-date earned premium for life insurance, plus
2. _________ percent (____%) of the inception-to-date earned premium for disability insurance, less
3. Inception-to-date incurred claims, or 15% of earned premiums, whichever is greater, less
4. Inception-to-date commissions paid under the Agency Agreements, less
5. All Retroactive Compensation previously paid.

B. If the combined remainder computed in Paragraph A is a plus figure, the Company shall pay to the Agent within thirty (30) days the amount of such remainder provided that all premiums then due the Company shall have been received by the Company. The total compensation to be paid under this Addendum shall not exceed the maximum amount promulgated by the insurance statutes and regulations of the state wherein the business is written.
Should the combined remainder computed in Paragraph A be a minus figure, the minus figure shall be carried over to subsequent accountings against any amounts that otherwise become payable to the Agent under the aforesaid formula. Company reserves the right to require Agent to repay any retroactive compensation received because of errors in calculations or in the event of retroactive reductions in premium rates.

C. Notwithstanding the provisions of the above, it is specifically understood and agreed that this Addendum shall be effective only for calendar years that Agent shall write for Company a combined

Figure 4.1. Sample retroactive compensation agreement

annual premium of not less than ______________ Dollars ($____________) for all types of insurance. In the event an accounting is performed for a period of time other than a full calendar year, the minimum required premium to make this Addendum effective will be determined by dividing the above figure by twelve (12) and then multiplying the result by the number of full months in the accounting period.

D. It is a condition precedent to payment of any additional compensation by Company that agent shall certify in writing to the Company that all known claims have been reported to Company. It is understood and agreed, however, that no waiver of this condition precedent shall result should the Company fail to require such certification of claims.

E. In the event of termination of this Agreement, the Company need not make further payment nor accountings of retroactive compensation to the Agent until such time as all liabilities including unearned premiums and losses and adjustment expenses, arising out of policies and/or certificates issued pursuant to this Agreement shall have been terminated by expiration, cancellation, payment or settlement, as the case may be. In the event of termination of this Agreement, and during the expiration of all policies and/or certificates in force, should the combined remainder computed in Paragraph A be a minus figure, it is understood and agreed that the Agent shall Hold Harmless and reimburse the Company in the amount of the minus figure (not to exceed the amounts previously paid under this Addendum) within thirty (30) days from receipt of demand by Company.

II. AGENT ACCOUNTS

This Retroactive Compensation Addendum shall be applicable to those accounts set forth at Exhibit A which is attached hereto and incorporated by reference.

Executed on behalf of the Company at ____________, the ___ day of __________, 19___.

By:____________________
Title:__________________

Executed by or on behalf of the Agent at ____________, this ___ day of __________, 19___.

________________________

By:____________________
Title:__________________

Figure 4.1. Sample retroactive compensation agreement

a retro calculation is done annually on the anniversary of the inception date, but each successive calculation includes all business since the inception date.

After profit is determined and allocated between the dealership and the insurer, any prior retro payments must be deducted. The amount that shows up as profit in an inception-to-date calculation is the accumulated profit, so it is necessary for the insurer to deduct any prior profits that have already been paid to the dealership. Figure 4.2 at the end of the chapter shows examples of ITD retro calculations.

A second method of calculation may be used, but it produces the same net result. These accountings cover the specific time period of the retro calculation, a **period retro**. For instance, if an annual retro is calculated on a policy with a January 1 effective date, the items will show only the amounts for the particular calendar year. Figure 4.3 shows examples of a period retro calculation.

Under this method, the contract will require that losses be carried forward. If the accounting produces a positive amount, it is paid to the dealership. If the result is a negative, it is carried forward and deducted from the next positive payment. If the negatives continue until all business expires, the insurer must absorb the loss.

Some contracts require that the dealership pay back any prior retros when there are negatives. Assume the dealership receives $10,000 in retros in its first two retro calculations. If the third calculation has a loss of $12,000, the dealership would be required to pay back the $10,000. It would never be required to pay back more than the $10,000; its cumulative cash can never be less than zero.

The general formula for a retro calculation is:

Earned premiums
less Incurred claims
less Front compensation
less Administrative fee
= Profit

## Earned Premiums

Even though the single premium is collected up front, it is not included in net income immediately. The cash has been collected, but the insurance protection has not been provided. As the insurance protection is provided during the policy term, the original single premium is **earned**. This is decreasing term insurance; more insurance is provided during the early policy months, so more premium is earned in the early policy months. For a 48-month policy, the approximate proportion of the premium earned each year is:

| Policy Year | Percentage of Single Premium Earned in Each Policy Year |
|---|---|
| 1 | 50% |
| 2 | 30% |
| 3 | 15% |
| 4 | 5% |
| Total | 100% |

The calculation must be done certificate by certificate, but with today's computers, this is a simple task. On each certificate in force on the calculation date, an **unearned premium** will be calculated. This is the portion of the original premium that has yet to be earned. In other words, it is approximately the premium that would be charged for the coverage that has yet to be provided.

The difference between the original premium and the unearned premium is the **earned premium**. This is the portion of the original premium used for the insurance that has already been provided. The insurer is off this risk and can consider the premium dollars earned.

When a refund occurs, the unearned premium is paid to the insured, and the insured's record is removed from the inforce records. In future calculations, the unearned premium is zero, but the refunds paid out in cash must be deducted from the original cash premiums that were collected.

In an inception-to-date accounting, the formula is:

  Gross written premiums
- Premium refunds
= Net written premiums

  Net written premiums
- (Unearned premiums at the end of the period)
= Inception-to-date earned premiums

In a period retro, the formula is:

  Gross written premiums
- Premium refunds
= Net written premiums

  Net written premiums
+ (Unearned premiums
  at the beginning of the period)
- (Unearned premiums
  at the end of the period)
= Earned premiums for the period

The two formulas are really identical. The beginning unearned premium is always zero in an ITD accounting, and the "period" is from inception.

## Incurred Claims

Just as premiums are calculated on an **accrual basis** rather than a cash basis, incurred claims include more than just paid claims.

The inception-to-date accounting formula is:

  Cash claims
+ Claim reserves at the end of the period
= Inception-to-date incurred claims

The period formula is:

  Cash claims
- Claim reserves at the beginning of the period
+ Claim reserves at the end of the period
= Incurred claims for the period

Again, the formulas are identical. The beginning claim reserves are always zero in an ITD accounting.

It is clear that cash claims must be deducted; the reason for claim reserves is more difficult to explain. The simple answer is that this is the rule for accrual accounting. The calculation includes all of the premiums earned up to and including the accounting date. For a proper accounting, we must include the *full cost* of all claims that have occurred on or before the accounting date. Claims that have occurred and have been paid are paid claims. But some claims have occurred that have not been paid. Also, on disability claims, additional payments will be earned by claimants after the accounting date on claims that are currently in a claim status.

**A claim reserve must include all payments to be made after the accounting date on any claim that occurred on or before the accounting date. Insurance companies are required by law to compute this number as accurately as possible and to maintain the reserve.**

There are three categories of claim reserves:

- **Incurred But Not Reported (IBNR)**
- **Claims in Course of Settlement (CCS)**
- **Continuing Claim Reserve (CCR) (disability only)**

An example of an IBNR claim is one that occurs just before the accounting date. The claim has occurred, but it has not been reported to the insurance company. At some point in the future, this claim will be reported to the insurer and subsequently paid.

A CCS claim is one that has been received by the insurer on the accounting date but has not been completely processed, so a payment has not been made. For example, if a death has been reported to the insurance company but the death certificate has not been received, the insurance company must establish a reserve for this claim which is in course of settlement.

For disability claims, those currently receiving claim benefits will receive additional benefits if they remain disabled after the accounting date—as most of them will. The estimate of these future claim payments is included in the claim reserves as a CCR amount.

The calculation of all of these amounts involves estimation. Actuaries study past claims and measure the relationship between the date claims occur and when the actual payments are disbursed. The primary method is to select an accounting date in the past and keep track of all payments made after the accounting date on all claims that happened on or before the accounting date. Insurers expend a great deal of effort to determine claim reserves.

The distinction among the three categories is not important—it's the total of all three that is critical. Some insurers show just one amount for claim reserves, while others separate the total into one or more of the categories.

On most business, the level of claim reserves will significantly affect the amount of retros that are paid. Each insurer's business is unique. The level of reserves for an insurer depends on the timing between when its claims occur and when they are paid, and on the average time its claimants remain disabled.

Generally, the total claim reserves for life insurance are about equal to three months of average claim payments. This rule of thumb applies unless there is a large claim that is being processed on the accounting date.

Claim reserves for disability are much larger. The total can equal or exceed 14 months of claim payments. This factor has been increasing steadily for the last 15 years. There has been a steady increase in the average duration of disability claims as the term of automobile loans has moved from 36 months in the 1970s to the current level of 60 months in many cases. The policies are longer, so a long-term claim has longer to run and earn benefits. While the level of claim reserves may seem suspicious at first, rest assured that the numbers are valid. These factors will be even higher for the first two years of a new block of business. Upon entering into a reinsurance program, a dealer will see that some claims continue for many years. Most insurers are willing to provide data on the dealership's claims, so actual payments can be seen.

## Compensation

The major distinction between retro programs is the timing by which compensation is deducted. The first method is to deduct the commissions that are **paid**. There is no standard term for this type of retro, but the term "retro" alone usually implies this method. It is sometimes called a **statutory retro** (see Chapter 6). The telling characteristic is that paid (written) commissions are deducted.

Charging paid commissions against earned premium slows down the payment of retros. In most cases, business must be written for two years or more before profits emerge.

The alternative method is to deduct earned commissions. In these retros, commissions are calculated by multiplying the earned premium times the front commission percentage. Just as premiums are earned over the term of the policies, commissions are charged over the term of the policies. These are called **GAAP retros** (GAAP meaning Generally Accepted Accounting Principles). With GAAP retros, it is possible to receive a retro payment from the first retro calculation. However, most insurers require a contingency reserve or holdback under GAAP retros. The insurer must protect against future unfavorable experience. Depending on the level of contingency reserves, the actual cash flow may not be much different from a statutory retro.

### Administrative Fees

Finally, the insurer will deduct an **administrative fee**. It is often called a **retention**. This fee will include the insurer's general operating expenses, profit margin, and risk margin. It may include premium taxes (generally 2% or 2.5% of net written premium), or taxes may be a separate item.

When dealing through a general agent, the dealership must remember that the agent is being compensated for the services he provides. A general agent's compensation is a percentage of premium called an **override commission**. In some cases this may be shown in the compensation section along with the dealership's front commission, but the normal practice is to include it in the insurer's administrative fee.

Administrative fees span a wide range of percentages and, again, they are only one element in a total retro program. One major influence is the annual volume of business produced by the dealership. As volume increases, administrative fees go down. Dealerships producing less than $100,000 a year in premium often have fees from 15% to 20% plus premium taxes. From $100,000 to $250,000 the fees range from 10% to 15% plus taxes. Above $250,000, each deal is separately negotiated, and the fees may drop below 10%.

The range of fees reflects economies of scale and risk factors. It costs the same to set up all new accounts. The cost of processing a premium report is almost the same regardless of the amount of business being submitted. Many other costs do not vary with volume or are marginally more expensive. As in the automobile business, volume counts.

Of equal concern is the risk factor. The larger the volume of business, the more predictable and stable the loss experience becomes. The insurer is primarily worried about paying out retros for a few years and then seeing the profits on the block go negative. The likelihood of this happening is far greater on a smaller volume than on a larger volume. Therefore, on smaller accounts, the insurer will charge a higher risk fee, since it must recover some money from the positive accounts to offset the accounts that go negative.

Along these lines, insurers may impose minimums that must be met before the first retro is paid. The contract may specify that the first retro calculation will not be paid until business has been written for 18-24 months. Alternatively, it may not pay any retro until earned premiums exceed a specified level, say $50,000. These conditions are imposed to give the business a chance to season a bit.

## TERMINATION PROVISION

It would be wonderful to think that the relationship with the insurer will go on forever. Many of the provisions would lose their importance—GAAP versus statutory, minimum earned premium requirements, the level of claim reserves, etc. If business continues long enough, all of these items will wash out.

But such blissful relationships are the exception rather than the rule. Since 1980, the profit margins for credit insurers have been low (1979 was the high-water mark for both volume and profits when measured in constant dollars). The result has been a revolving door of insurers getting in and out of the business.

As the prima facie rates and interest rates have dropped since 1980, insurers had to reduce compensation. Dealers moved business from one insurer to the next in an effort to maintain existing commission levels. The 1980s was a volatile decade for dealerships also. There were few dealership-insurer relationships that spanned the decade.

Most retro programs provide that if the dealership terminates the relationship with the insurer, all retro payments stop immediately. Many programs include the provision that even if the insurer cancels the dealership, the retro program stops after the next retro calculation. These are often called **walkaway retros**.

If a retro program is positive and producing profits, the likelihood is that the business already on the books will produce further profits as the business runs off. If a dealer is on a statutory program, the future profits could be substantial. The calculation shown in Figure 4.4 should be made to estimate the value of future retros on the business that has already been produced. This is the economic cost of leaving the current insurer and must be judged against the impetus for the switch. Switching carriers leaves **MONEY ON THE TABLE**.

A slightly more favorable termination provision is that the insurer will make a final termination retro payment when all of the business expires. Some insurers include this provision when the insurer cancels the dealership, but retros still stop if the dealership cancels the insurer. This sounds good, but it will be five to seven years before all business expires. The dealer should mark his calendar and ask the insurer to continue to provide occasional accountings.

The most favorable provision is that retro payments continue periodically until all business expires. Few insurers grant this provision. They want the dealer to think twice about leaving them. In addition, they must incur the cost of continuing to do the calculations while the dealer is now someone else's customer.

Overall, the insurer owns the business that has been written and takes the position that it will share the profits with the dealer as long as the dealer is writing new business. This is a fundamental difference between retro programs and reinsurance programs. Under most reinsurance programs, it's the dealer's business, and he has rights to it until it expires.

## EXAMPLES

These examples show how retro balances emerge based on two years of production and then runoff to demonstrate the effect of the different methods. In actual practice, any positive balances payable would be subject to the termination provision.

Figure 4.2 ITD Statutory Retro
All amounts are cumulative from the inception of the contract. For life insurance, the policy reserves may be unearned premium reserves (UPR) or mortality reserves (see Chapter 5). The front commissions and administrative fees deducted are a percentage of net written premiums.

Figure 4.2 ITD GAAP Retro
All amounts are cumulative from the inception of the contract. Unearned premiums are always used in the calculations. The front commissions and administrative fees deducted are a percentage of earned premiums.

Figure 4.3 Period Statutory Retro
All amounts are for the year. The change in policy reserves is the difference between the ITD ending reserves for the current year and the ITD ending reserves for the prior year.

Figure 4.3 Period GAAP Retro
All amounts are for the year. The change in policy reserves is the difference between the ITD ending reserves for the year and the ITD ending reserves for the prior year.

## Formulas for Figure 4.4

Refund percentage = (refunds)/(earned premiums)

This formula will produce a slightly different result from the answer shown. The answer shown is adjusted to produce the same dollars as the examples where the future refunds were known.

Loss ratio percentage =
(incurred claims)/(earned premiums)

Future earned premiums =
{1 - (refund percentage)} x (ending policy reserves)

Profit margin

Statutory = {1 - (loss ratio)}

All commissions and administrative fees have already been charged off.

GAAP = {1 - (loss ratio) - (front commission percentage) - (administrative fee percentage)};

If administrative fees are deducted on a statutory basis, remove the administrative fee percentage from the formula.

Future profits = (profit margin) x (future earned premiums)

Gain on refunds (statutory only) = (refunds) x { (front commission percentage) + (administrative fee percentage)}

On a refund, $1.00 of unearned premium is released, but the cash paid is net of the front commissions and administrative fees that have already been expensed in a statutory retro.

Note: The final amount for the statutory column ($8,300) differs from the final result shown in Figure 4.2 and Figure 4.3 ($8,306) due to rounding. For the same reason, future GAAP profits ($4,461) in Figure 4.4 is slightly different from the amounts in Figure 4.2 and Figure 4.3 ($4,466).

| INCEPTION-TO-DATE STATUTORY RETRO | | | | | | |
|---|---|---|---|---|---|---|
| | Year 1 | Year 2 | Year 3 | Year 4 | Years 5-6 | Total |
| Gross Written Premiums | 100,000 | 200,000 | 200,000 | 200,000 | 200,000 | 200,000 |
| Refunds | 5,070 | 17,009 | 27,852 | 32,783 | 33,872 | 33,872 |
| Net Written Premiums | 94,930 | 182,991 | 172,148 | 167,217 | 166,128 | 166,128 |
| Ending Policy Reserves | 71,925 | 106,204 | 46,311 | 13,718 | 0 | 0 |
| Earned Premiums | 23,005 | 76,787 | 125,837 | 153,499 | 166,128 | 166,128 |
| Front Commissions | 33,226 | 64,047 | 60,252 | 58,526 | 58,145 | 58,145 |
| Administrative Fees | 18,986 | 36,598 | 34,430 | 33,443 | 33,226 | 33,226 |
| Incurred Claims | 9,202 | 30,715 | 55,335 | 61,400 | 66,451 | 66,451 |
| Balance-To-Date | (38,409) | (54,573) | (24,180) | 130 | 8,306 | 8,306 |
| Less Prior Paid | 0 | 0 | 0 | 0 | 130 | 0 |
| Retro Payable | 0 | 0 | 0 | 130 | 8,176 | 8,306 |

| INCEPTION-TO-DATE GAAP RETRO | | | | | | |
|---|---|---|---|---|---|---|
| | Year 1 | Year 2 | Year 3 | Year 4 | Years 5-6 | Total |
| Gross Written Premiums | 100,000 | 200,000 | 200,000 | 200,000 | 200,000 | 200,000 |
| Refunds | 5,070 | 17,009 | 27,852 | 32,783 | 33,872 | 33,872 |
| Net Written Premiums | 94,930 | 182,991 | 172,148 | 167,217 | 166,128 | 166,128 |
| Change in UEP Reserves | 71,925 | 106,204 | 46,311 | 13,718 | 0 | 0 |
| Earned Premiums | 23,005 | 76,787 | 125,837 | 153,499 | 166,128 | 166,128 |
| Front Commissions | 8,052 | 26,875 | 44,043 | 53,725 | 58,145 | 58,145 |
| Administrative Fees | 4,601 | 15,357 | 25,167 | 30,700 | 33,226 | 33,226 |
| Incurred Claims | 9,202 | 30,715 | 55,335 | 61,400 | 66,451 | 66,451 |
| Balance-To-Date | 1,150 | 3,840 | 1,292 | 7,674 | 8,306 | 8,306 |
| Less Prior Paid | 0 | 1,150 | 3,840 | 3,840 | 7,674 | 0 |
| Retro Payable | 1,150 | 2,690 | 0 | 3,834 | 632 | 8,306 |

All amounts are cumulative from inception.
Policy reserves equal unearned premiums.
Assumptions: Front Commissions 35%, Ultimate loss ratio 40%
Administrative fees (including premium taxes) 20%

Figure 4.2. Inception-to-date retro examples

| PERIOD STATUTORY RETRO | | | | | | |
|---|---|---|---|---|---|---|
| | Year 1 | Year 2 | Year 3 | Year 4 | Years 5-6 | Total |
| Gross Written Premiums | 100,000 | 100,000 | 0 | 0 | 0 | 200,000 |
| Refunds | 5,070 | 11,939 | 10,843 | 4,931 | 1,089 | 33,872 |
| Net Written Premiums | 94,930 | 88,061 | (10,843) | (4,931) | (1,089) | 166,128 |
| Change in Policy Res. | 71,925 | 34,279 | (59,893) | (32,593) | (13,718) | 0 |
| "Earned Premiums" | 23,005 | 53,782 | 49,050 | 27,662 | 12,629 | 166,128 |
| Front Commissions | 33,226 | 30,821 | (3,795) | (1,726) | (381) | 58,145 |
| Administrative Fees | 18,986 | 17,612 | (2,168) | (987) | (217) | 33,226 |
| Incurred Claims | 9,202 | 21,513 | 24,620 | 6,065 | 5,051 | 66,451 |
| Balance For Year | (38,409) | (16,164) | 30,393 | 24,310 | 8,176 | 8,306 |
| Loss Carryforward | 0 | (38,409) | (54,573) | (24,180) | 130 | 0 |
| Retro Payable | 0 | 0 | 0 | 130 | 8,306 | 8,306 |

| PERIOD GAAP RETRO | | | | | | |
|---|---|---|---|---|---|---|
| | Year 1 | Year 2 | Year 3 | Year 4 | Years 5-6 | Total |
| Gross Written Premiums | 100,000 | 100,000 | 0 | 0 | 0 | 200,000 |
| Refunds | 5,070 | 11,939 | 10,843 | 4,931 | 1,089 | 33,872 |
| Net Written Premiums | 94,930 | 88,061 | (10,843) | (4,931) | (1,089) | 166,128 |
| Change in UEP Reserves | 71,925 | 34,279 | (59,893) | (32,593) | (13,718) | 0 |
| Earned Premiums | 23,005 | 53,782 | 49,050 | 27,662 | 12,629 | 166,128 |
| Front Commissions | 8,052 | 18,823 | 17,168 | 9,682 | 4,420 | 58,145 |
| Administrative Fees | 4,601 | 10,756 | 9,810 | 5,533 | 2,526 | 33,226 |
| Incurred Claims | 9,202 | 21,513 | 24,620 | 6,065 | 5,051 | 66,451 |
| Balance For Year | 1,150 | 2,690 | (2,548) | 6,382 | 632 | 8,306 |
| Loss Carryforward | 0 | 0 | 0 | 2,548 | 0 | 0 |
| Retro Payable | 1,150 | 2,690 | 0 | 3,834 | 632 | 8,306 |

All amounts represent the experience for the year.
Policy reserves equal unearned premiums.
Assumptions: Front commissions 35%, Ultimate loss ratio 40%
Administrative fees (including premium taxes) 20%

Figure 4.3. Period retro examples

| WALKAWAY RETRO | | | | | |
|---|---|---|---|---|---|
| These calculations are based on terminating the retro contract after the second year using the data in the preceding examples. Amounts are inception-to-date. | | | | | |
| **Line** | **Item** | **Formula** | **Statutory Retro** | | **GAAP Retro** |
| a | Gross Written Premiums | | 200,000 | | 200,000 |
| b | Refunds | | 17,009 | | 17,009 |
| c | Net Written Premiums | a - b | 182,991 | | 182,991 |
| d | Ending Policy Reserves | | 106,204 | | 106,204 |
| e | Earned Premiums to Date | c - d | 76,787 | | 76,787 |
| f | Incurred Claims to Date | | 30,715 | | 30,715 |
| g | Refund Percentage | | 16% | | 16% |
| h | Loss Ratio Percentage | f / e | 40% | | 40% |
| i | Future Earned Premiums | (1 - g) * d | 89,211 | | 89,211 |
| j | Future Profit Margin<br>GAAP: (1-h)-cr-af<br>cr = commission rate<br>af = administrative fees | 1 - h | 0.60 | | 0.05 |
| k | Future Profits | j * i | 53,527 | | 4,461 |
| l | Gain on Refunds | (cr+af)*(d-i) | 9,346 | | N/A |
| m | Loss Carryforward | Year 2 | (54,573) | | 0 |
| n | **Expected Future Profits** | **k + l + m** | **8,300** | | **4,461** |

**MONEY LEFT ON THE TABLE**

Figure 4.4. Walkaway retro calculations

# Chapter Five
# Reinsurance

An understanding of the concepts of reinsurance begins with the basics of insurance itself. In return for the single premium, the insurance company issues a policy which provides a defined set of benefits. This company, the **direct writer**, is the company whose name is on the policy. Regardless of any reinsurance, the direct writer is responsible to the insured for the payment of a claim.

## THE RISK OF INSURANCE

Everyone knows that insurance companies are risk-taking enterprises, but the actual risk undertaken is often misunderstood. The real role of insurance companies is to spread risk. By taking a small premium from many people, the insurance company can provide a substantial benefit to the few who have claims. The risk of insurance is not that there will be claims. No one panics in the claims department when the mail is opened and there is a claim inside. Instead, the risk of insurance is that the insurance company will not correctly estimate the magnitude of claims that will happen.

Predicting the level of claims is the role of actuaries. It is their job to estimate the amount of claims and to set adequate premium rates. These premium rates must be adequate to pay claims and provide for expenses and profits. In credit insurance, the premium rate is effectively set by the state, so the role of the actuary is to set the commission levels.

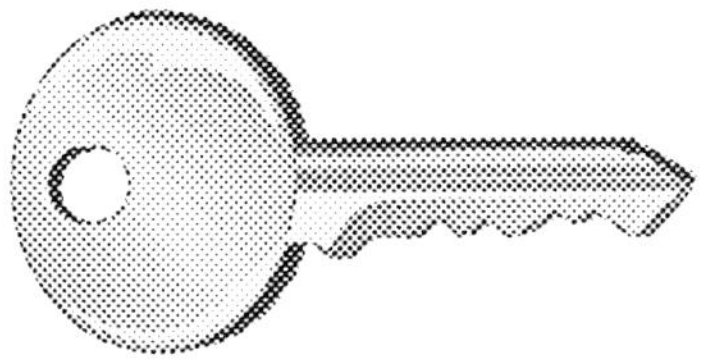

The key to successfully insuring the public is correctly estimating the number of claims.

The process of successfully predicting claim levels depends on several factors. First, there must be a significant number of insureds involved. Only a small percentage of insureds have claims. While the actuary never knows which people will have claims, given a sufficient number of insureds, the actuary can reasonably predict the magnitude of claims. Unfortunately, it takes a large number of insureds for the process to produce consistent results.

Another factor is timing. People do not die or become disabled on a consistent basis. Over a ten-year period, the actuary may accurately predict the magnitude of claims, but the estimate may be way off in the individual years. It is important for insurance companies to have the financial support to weather the years when an unusual number of claims occur.

For example, if a dealership produces $25,000 of credit life premium in a particular year, the ultimate profitability of this group of insureds can vary widely. Over the five years the policies are in force, the expected number of claims may be three, with an average claim of $5,000. For this small number of insureds, however, the actual number of claims could easily vary from zero to six. If there are no claims, the business is wildly profitable, but with six claims, the claim cost exceeds the premium. If this volume of business is written in each of ten years, there will be good years and bad years.

As the volume of business increases, the expected number of claims becomes more predictable, and the pattern becomes smoother. Still, even large insurance companies with millions of insureds have noticeable variations in claim experience from year to year.

## DEFINITIONS

**Reinsurance** is the transfer of risk from one insurance company to another. The process of reinsurance moves the insurance to the reinsurer. Still, the reinsurance creates an obligation of the reinsurer only to the direct writer. The direct writer retains all obligations to the insured.

The direct writer is said to **cede** the business and becomes the **ceding company**. The reinsurer is said to **assume** the business and becomes the **assuming company** or **reinsurer**.

If the reinsurer transfers part or all of the risk to a second reinsurer, it is said to **retrocede** the business. The second reinsurer again **assumes** the business and becomes the **retrocessionaire**.

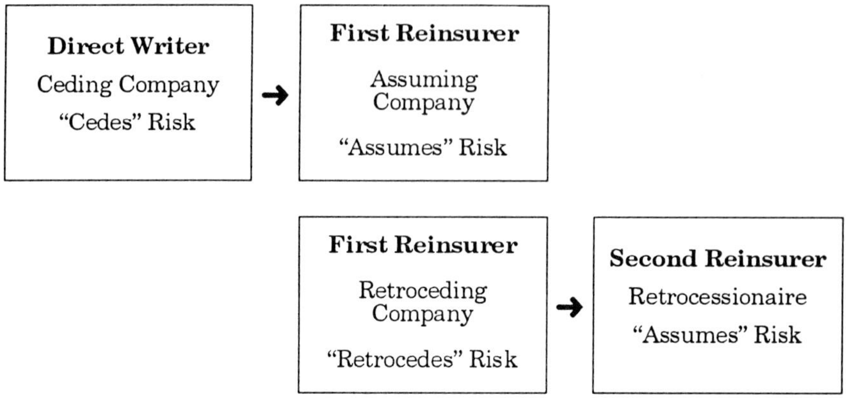


In actual reinsurance operations, the ceding company provides monthly or quarterly reports of the business processed to the assuming company. These reports provide the details of the business ceded and are called **cessions**.

A **producer-owned reinsurer** is a reinsurance company owned or controlled by the party that is producing the business. A reinsurer owned by a dealer which assumes the credit insurance business produced by that dealership is a producer-owned reinsurer, or simply a reinsurer.

United States insurance regulations make a distinction between a *life insurance company* and a *casualty insurance company*. Relative to dealership-sold insurance products, a life insurance company can underwrite only credit life and disability policies. A casualty insurer can underwrite credit disability insurance but not life insurance. Service contract insurance is a casualty product and cannot be underwritten or reinsured by a life company.

In the Caribbean islands, there is only one category—an insurance company. Such a corporation can insure credit life and disability products, as well as service contracts.

To further complicate matters, there is also a distinction for federal income tax purposes between a life insurance company and a non-life (i.e., casualty) insurance company. The definitions for tax purposes are contained in the tax code and differ from the legal definitions. For example, a life insurance company that underwrites only credit disability insurance would be considered a non-life company for tax purposes. The tax classification of an insurer that writes life and non-life products depends on the proportion of business in each category. There are significant differences in the tax rates for life companies versus non-life companies.

| Product | Type of Insurance Co. Required (U.S.) | Type of Insurance Co. Required (Caribbean) | Category For Federal Income Tax |
|---|---|---|---|
| Credit Life | Life Insurer | Ins. Co. | Life Ins. |
| Credit Disability | Either | Ins. Co. | Non-life |
| Service Contracts | Casualty | Ins. Co. | Non-life |

All of these classifications also apply to reinsurance companies. In most state laws and regulations and in the tax code, reinsurers must meet or exceed the same minimum reserve requirements and other regulations as direct writers.

## REINSURANCE TREATIES

The reinsurance relationship is defined by a contract between the direct writer and the reinsurer called a **reinsurance treaty**. This 10- to 20-page document spells out the rights and obligations of each party. Below are the typical sections of a reinsurance treaty and the purpose of each.

*Parties to the Contract.* Contains the full legal name and location of each party and defines each party's role.

*Insuring Clause.* Contains a general description of the risks reinsured, the form of reinsurance and the coinsurance percentage. It often references a schedule or attachment with the details of the risks reinsured.

*Premium Clause.* Contains the definition of the basis of premiums and the period of remittance.

*Claims Clause.* Contains the definition of the basis of claims and the period of reimbursement.

*Expense Clause.* Contains the expenses which the direct writer will deduct from the premiums ceded.

*Reports Clause.* Contains the details of the reports which the direct writer will provide and the timing of reports and remittances.

*Oversight Clause.* Provides that unintentional errors will be corrected and that parties will be placed in the same position as if the oversight had not occurred.

*Inspection Clause.* Provides that the reinsurer has the right to inspect all records of the direct writer relating to the reinsured policies at reasonable times.

*Insolvency Clause.* Provides that the reinsurance is payable to the ceding company even if the ceding company becomes insolvent or is placed in conservatorship.

*Arbitration Clause*. Provides that any dispute between the ceding company and the assuming company be settled by arbitration rather than court action.

## Ceding Fees

In return for its administration, the direct writer will charge the reinsurer an administration fee which is a percentage of premium. This fee provides for the general expenses of the direct writer in processing the business. It also includes a profit and risk margin.

The preferred name for the administrative charge is the **ceding fee**. It says what it is—a fee for the ceding of the business. Some companies in the industry still use the term **retention**. There is nothing wrong with the term—it represents the portion of the premium that is retained by the direct writer. However, the term has a broader meaning in the life insurance industry. (In the general usage, an insurer's retention is the maximum risk that the insurer will retain on any one life. An insurer with a $50,000 retention will buy stop-loss reinsurance for any amount that it insures on any one life in excess of $50,000.)

The fee may be a flat percentage of all premiums, but a scale of stepped percentages which vary based on annual production is common. Two types of stepped scales are in use. The more common scale applies a lower percentage to incremental production. For example:

15% of the first $1,000,000
plus 12% of the next $1,000,000
plus 10% of the excess over $2,000,000

If a dealership produces $4,000,000 of annual premium, the fee would be:

| | |
|---|---|
| .15 x 1,000,000 = | 150,000 |
| + .12 x 1,000,000 = | 120,000 |
| + .10 x 2,000,000 = | 200,000 |
| Total | $470,000 |

A retroactive scale applies the lower percentage to all business if certain production levels are met; for example:

15% if annual production is less than $1,000,000
12% if production is greater than $1,000,000 and less than $2,000,000
10% if production is greater than $2,000,000

At the $4,000,000 production level, the fee would be:

.10 x 4,000,000 = $400,000

Both types recognize that the direct writer has certain fixed expenses with each reinsurance program, but some expenses vary. Because there are many fixed expenses, a direct writer has significant economies of scale associated with larger volume levels.

Some of the fixed expenses include policy form filing, preparation of reinsurance treaties, and periodic cessions. Premium booking is semi-fixed. It costs only slightly more to book a $10,000 report than it does a $1,000 report. Claim processing is primarily variable—as business increases, claims increase.

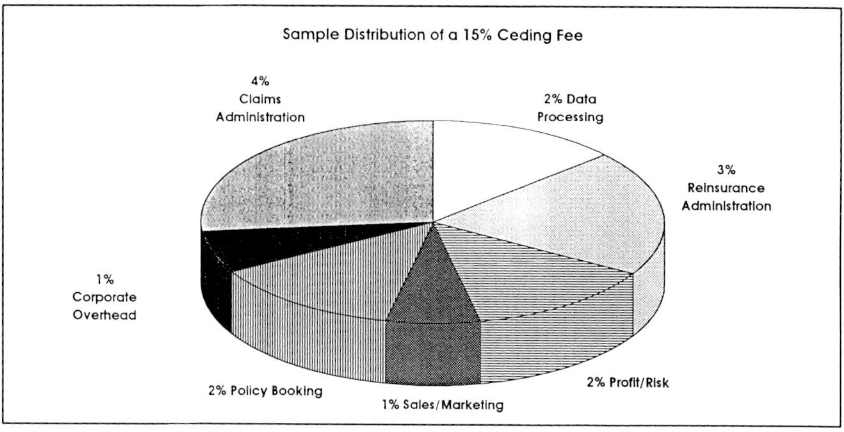


## Premium Taxes

Direct writers pay premium taxes in almost all states where policies are issued. This expense is recovered from the reinsurer. Since the cost is a percentage of net written premium, it may be included in the ceding fee. Most ceding fees, however, do not include premium taxes. There is either a separate charge based on a stated percentage or just a pass-through expense for actual premium taxes paid.

While this appears to be an obligatory expense, remember that direct writers may not pay the same premium tax rate for business written in a particular state. Two facets of premium tax regulation affect the cost—**discriminatory domicile rates** and **retaliatory taxes**.

An insurance company is formed in one state—its state of **domicile**. It is then licensed to do business in other states, where it is a **foreign** company. A number of states levy lower premium tax rates on their domestic companies. An example is Ohio. An Ohio domestic does not pay any premium tax on business written in Ohio, while all foreign companies pay a 2.5% premium tax rate. This is often called the "favorite son premium tax" statute. This gives favorable tax treatment to domiciled companies.

Then there are retaliatory rates. For foreign companies, most states specify that the rate levied is the higher of:

- The state premium tax rate for foreign companies, or

- The rate charged its domestic companies by the foreign company's state of domicile.

For example, Arizona has a 2% premium tax rate for foreign companies. But a foreign company domiciled in Ohio must pay 2.5%—the rate that Ohio would charge a company domiciled in Arizona for business written in Ohio.

Retaliatory Premium Tax

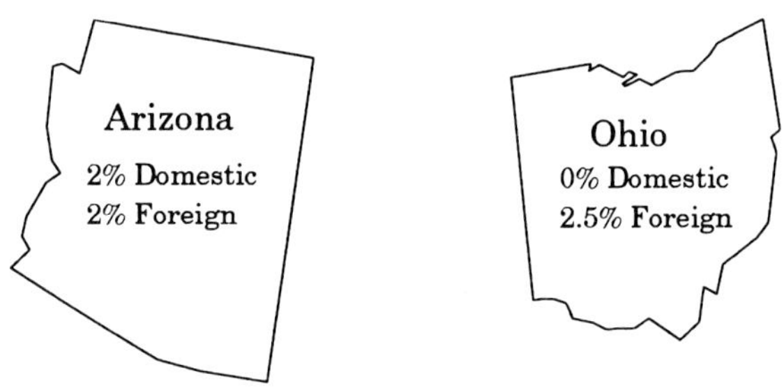

An Ohio domiciled insurer pays 2.5% tax in Arizona due to the retaliatory tax law.

The bottom line is that premium taxes vary by state and by direct writer within the state. A reinsurer comparing the ceding fees between two direct writers should include premium taxes in the comparison.

### Other Fees

Most direct writers levy some additional fees to reflect the growing problem of regulatory assessments and unusual expenses. Treaties specify that the reinsurer will be charged for any guaranty fund assessment or other levies by state regulatory authorities where the reinsurer's business affects the amount levied on the direct writer. For example, guaranty fund assessments are often allocated among the direct writers of a state based on premium written.

A second category of special fees applies to extraordinary out-of-pocket costs for claims investigation. These are costs over and above normal claim processing. Since the reinsurer is the expected beneficiary of a reduced claim amount, it is expected to pay the unusual costs.

## TYPES OF REINSURANCE

There are two types of reinsurance which are found in producer-owned reinsurance. **Coinsurance**, or **quota share reinsurance**, is the basic form of most reinsurance. Lacking any description to the contrary, one can assume that the terms *producer-owned reinsurance* and *coinsurance* are synonymous. A second form, called **excess reinsurance**, or **stop-loss reinsurance**, is occasionally used in conjunction with coinsurance when the reinsurer desires to limit its risk on any one life or on its entire book of business.

The terms "coinsurance" and "quota share reinsurance" imply that the original risk is now split between the direct writer and the reinsurer. When there is a split, a **coinsurance percentage** will be specified in the reinsurance treaty. It defines the percentage of the original risk that is ceded to the reinsurer. A coinsurance percentage of 70% says that 70% of the risk is ceded to the reinsurer. In most arrangements, the reinsurer receives 70% of all elements of income and expense. It receives 70% of premiums less 70% of the claims, premium taxes, front commissions and other out-of-pocket expenses the direct writer incurs. In the accounting, there is also a deduction for the direct writer's ceding fee.

In producer-owned reinsurance, it is common for the coinsurance percentage to be 100%. All of the risk is ceded to the reinsurer. The reinsurer receives 100% of the premium less 100% of the claims and expenses.

To evaluate a coinsurance arrangement, one must understand the two forms of coinsurance—the **written basis** and **the earned basis**. Both are commonly used in producer-owned credit reinsurance programs. Often, a particular program will have a portion ceded on a written basis and a portion ceded on an earned basis.

The risk that is transferred is the same under both bases; let's assume the coinsurance percentage is 100%. All of the risk is transferred—only the timing of the cash flow is different. This timing difference, however, has dramatic implications for the actual profit earned by the reinsurer and for the reinsurer's accounting, taxation and regulatory positions.

## Earned Coinsurance

To understand the differences, it is easier to begin with earned coinsurance. Earned coinsurance is exactly like a GAAP retro described in Chapter 4—**except that, if the accounting is negative, the reinsurer must reimburse the ceding company for the loss.**

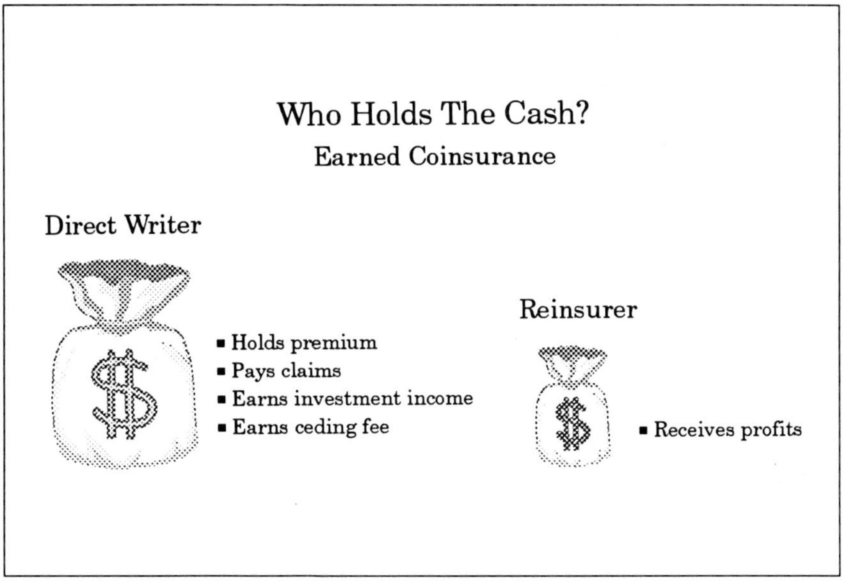


In general, a GAAP retro is just as advantageous as earned reinsurance. But there are three reasons for entering into such a reinsurance arrangement.

- In most states with commission caps, earned reinsurance is a legal method to have total earnings in excess of the cap.

- Reimbursement is more frequent than retros, which are generally paid annually.

- The direct writer may charge a ceding fee for earned reinsurance that is less than the administrative fee included in the retro calculation.

If the business is profitable, the earned reinsurance will produce profits that equal or exceed the profits under the GAAP retro arrangement.

As with retros, **the direct writer holds the cash until the profits emerge and earns the investment income**. While this is a real negative from the income standpoint, it does make for a simple reinsurance transaction. The reinsurer receives a periodic report of the business and a check for the earned profits. Since the reinsurer does not hold the cash, it does not need to set aside funds for future claims (reserves) nor does it need to establish a trust fund for this business.

## Written Coinsurance

In order for the reinsurer to capture the investment income and qualify as a life insurance company for federal income tax purposes, a portion of the life insurance business is ceded on a written basis. While the advantages are evident, this method does introduce some complications.

For business ceded on a written basis, the cash transactions—premiums, claims, ceding fees, expenses—move immediately to the reinsurer. With its single premium structure, credit insurance generates a substantial cash flow. Much of this cash flow will be needed in the future to pay claims. For that reason, the direct writer places controls on the funds. A custodial trust fund or letter of credit (LOC) is required. Contained in the agreement for the custodial trust are limitations on the way the funds may be invested. These requirements and conditions reflect restrictions and regulations imposed on the direct writer and are good business practice. The direct writer must pay the claims to the insured; therefore, it must guarantee that the funds are available from the reinsurer for reimbursement.

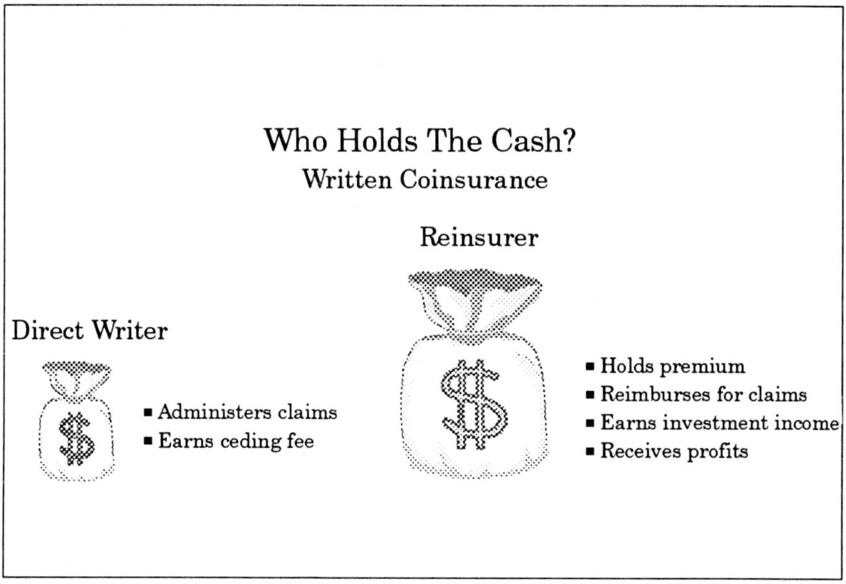


The following pages show a comparison of the actual cash flow under each form of coinsurance. Appendix C contains a sample reinsurance treaty with both forms of coinsurance.

## Excess Reinsurance

**Excess Reinsurance** serves to protect the producer-owned reinsurer from large claims on any one life. It is also known as **stop-loss insurance**. The direct writer may offer to retain the risk in excess of $15,000, or some other limit, on any one policy. This protects the reinsurer from swings in profitability as a result of a large claim.

The reinsurance may be structured as *pure excess* coverage or as *per policy* coinsurance. Consider a $40,000 decreasing life policy with a $15,000 excess limit. Under pure excess, the direct writer will retain any risk over $15,000, but its protection will cease when the amount of insurance in force drops below $15,000. Under per policy coinsurance, the coinsurance percentage is set for each policy. For the example, the direct writer would retain [(40,000-15,000)/40,000] or 62.5% of the risk on this policy. Whenever death occurs, the direct writer will be responsible for 62.5% of the claim.

The decision to participate in such a program is generally a financial toss-up. The dealership will still receive its front commission. The cost of claims on larger policies is higher than the usual business, since the average age of this group tends to be higher. Excess of $15,000 can be considered and excess of $25,000 is recommended if the direct writer provides the option. An excess program may be required for U.S. reinsurance programs, depending on the level of capital and surplus.

## Warehousing

Once a dealer decides a reinsurance program makes sense, a direct writer may **warehouse** the business for a period of time. This procedure recognizes that it may take up to six months for the dealer to form the reinsurance company, sign the reinsurance documents, and post any required cash. If the dealer agrees to a program effective May 1, the direct writer agrees to reinsure all business after April 30 once the reinsurer is up and running, i.e., it warehouses the business between May 1 and the date the reinsurer can accept business. It is normal for the direct writer to limit the period it will warehouse business to one year or less.

## EXAMPLES

Earned Reinsurance Program - Figure 5.1

After each ceding statement, the reinsurer receives or pays the amount due, which is equal to:

Earned Premiums
- Incurred Front Commissions
- Incurred Ceding Fees (and Premium Taxes)
- Incurred Claims

Front commissions, ceding fees and premium taxes are normally deducted based on the method of ceding the premium. On earned reinsurance, these are the incurred amounts shown. (The ceding fee is 17% of earned premium, including 2% for premium taxes.) Some direct writers deduct ceding fees on a paid (or written) basis.

For earned reinsurance, incurred claims are normally ceded; i.e., the direct writer holds the claim reserves. It is equally valid for the direct writer to cede paid claims. In this case, the reinsurer must establish the claim reserves as a liability and maintain the assets in the trust custodial account.

No investment income is generated, nor is a trust balance required, since the direct writer holds the cash supporting the unearned premiums and the claim reserves.

**Surplus drain** is created on the statutory books of the direct writer, but it is not passed on to the reinsurer.

The significant difference between earned reinsurance and a GAAP retro is demonstrated in year three. Under a GAAP retro the dealership has no liability; it simply does not receive any extra income for the period. The reinsurer, by contrast, must perform under the reinsurance treaty and reimburse the direct writer for the loss.

Written Reinsurance Program - Figure 5.2

After each ceding statement, the reinsurer receives or pays the amount due, which is equal to:

Net Written Premiums
- Paid Front Commissions
- Paid Ceding Fees (including Premium Taxes)
- Paid Claims

Front commissions, ceding fees, and premium taxes are almost always deducted on a paid basis, i.e., a percentage of net written premiums. Claims are normally deducted on a paid basis. (Some direct writers deduct incurred claims. If incurred claims are deducted, the direct writer holds the claim reserves, and this amount does not need to be maintained in the custodial trust account.) Significant cash flow is generated as long as new premiums are being produced.

The amount required in the custodial trust account is equal to the mortality reserves plus the claim reserves. This will normally exceed the cash received by the reinsurer in the first few years. The dealer must contribute additional surplus to the reinsurance company in order to maintain the minimum capital and surplus required by the regulators having jurisdiction over the reinsurer. Alternatively, some direct writers may not require the trust to exceed the cash received but charge a "surplus relief fee" because of the deficiency. This fee is about 5% (on an annual basis) times the amount of the deficiency.

The surplus drain is the cumulative statutory income. Note that profits in the example do not appear until the fourth year. The good news is that taxable income (which closely follows statutory income) also does not begin for a period of time.

EARNED REINSURANCE PROGRAM

**$100,000 of Gross Written Premium for Two Years then Runoff;**
**48-Month Term Policies**
**Front Commissions 35%, Ultimate Loss Ratio 40%**
**Ceding Fees (including Premium Taxes) 17%**
**Cash Items in italics**

| | | Year 1 | Year 2 | Year 3 | Year 4 | Years 5-6 | Total |
|---|---|---|---|---|---|---|---|
| | + Gross Written Premiums | 100,000 | 100,000 | 0 | 0 | 0 | 200,000 |
| | - Refunds | 5,070 | 11,939 | 10,843 | 4,931 | 1,089 | 33,872 |
| | = Net Written Premiums | 94,930 | 88,061 | (10,843) | (4,931) | (1,089) | 166,128 |
| | + Unearned Premiums-BOY | 0 | 71,925 | 106,204 | 46,311 | 13,718 | 0 |
| | - Unearned Premiums-EOY | 71,925 | 106,204 | 46,311 | 13,718 | 0 | 0 |
| + | = *Earned Premiums (EP)* | *23,005* | *53,782* | *49,050* | *27,662* | *12,629* | *166,128* |
| | + Front Commissions Paid | 33,226 | 30,821 | (3,795) | (1,726) | (381) | 58,145 |
| | + Unearned Front Costs-BOY | 0 | 25,174 | 37,172 | 16,209 | 4,801 | 0 |
| | - Unearned Front Costs-EOY | 25,174 | 37,172 | 16,209 | 4,801 | 0 | 0 |
| - | = *Earned Front Commissions* | *8,052* | *18,823* | *17,168* | *9,682* | *4,420* | *58,145* |
| - | *Earned Ceding Fees* | *3,911* | *9,143* | *8,339* | *4,703* | *2,147* | *28,243* |
| | + Paid Claims | 5,606 | 19,799 | 27,614 | 7,695 | 5,737 | 66,451 |
| | - Claim Reserves-BOY | 0 | 3,596 | 5,310 | 2,316 | 686 | 0 |
| | + Claim Reserves-EOY | 3,596 | 5,310 | 2,316 | 686 | 0 | 0 |
| - | = *Incurred Claims* | *9,202* | *21,513* | *24,620* | *6,065* | *5,051* | *66,451* |
| = | ***Amount Due Reinsurer*** | ***1,840*** | ***4,303*** | ***(1,077)*** | ***7,212*** | ***1,011*** | ***13,289*** |
| | Investment Income | 0 | 0 | 0 | 0 | 0 | 0 |
| | = **Statutory Net Income Before Tax** | **1,840** | **4,303** | **(1,077)** | **7,212** | **1,011** | **13,289** |
| | Required Trust Balance | 0 | 0 | 0 | 0 | 0 | 0 |
| | EOY Surplus Drain (Gain) | (1,840) | (6,143) | (5,066) | (12,278) | (13,289) | 0 |
| | **Total GAAP Income Before Tax** | **1,840** | **4,303** | **(1,077)** | **7,212** | **1,011** | **13,289** |

Figure 5.1. Earned reinsurance example.

**WRITTEN REINSURANCE PROGRAM**

**$100,000 of Gross Written Premium for Two Years then Runoff;**
**48-Month Term Policies**
**Front Commissions 35%, Ultimate Loss Ratio 40%**
**Ceding Fees (including Premium Taxes) 17%**
**Cash Items in italics**

| | | Year 1 | Year 2 | Year 3 | Year 4 | Years 5-6 | Total |
|---|---|---|---|---|---|---|---|
| | + *Gross Written Premium* | *100,000* | *100,000* | *0* | *0* | *0* | *200,000* |
| | - *Refunds* | *5,070* | *11,939* | *10,843* | *4,931* | *1,089* | *33,872* |
| + | = *Net Written Premium* | *94,930* | *88,061* | *(10,843)* | *(4,931)* | *(1,089)* | *166,128* |
| | + Unearned Premium-BOY | 0 | 71,925 | 106,204 | 46,311 | 13,718 | 0 |
| | - Unearned Premium-EOY | 71,925 | 106,204 | 46,311 | 13,718 | 0 | 0 |
| | = Earned Premium (EP) | 23,005 | 53,782 | 49,050 | 27,662 | 12,629 | 166,128 |
| - | + *Front Commissions Paid* | *33,226* | *30,821* | *(3,795)* | *(1,726)* | *(381)* | *58,145* |
| | + Unearned Front Costs-BOY | 0 | 25,174 | 37,172 | 16,209 | 4,801 | 0 |
| | - Unearned Front Costs-EOY | 25,174 | 37,172 | 16,209 | 4,801 | 0 | 0 |
| | = Earned Front Commissions | 8,052 | 18,823 | 17,168 | 9,682 | 4,420 | 58,145 |
| - | + *Ceding Fees* | *16,138* | *14,971* | *(1,843)* | *(838)* | *(185)* | *28,243* |
| | + Unearned Ceding Fees-BOY | 0 | 12,227 | 18,055 | 7,873 | 2,332 | 0 |
| | - Unearned Ceding Fees-EOY | 12,227 | 18,055 | 7,873 | 2,332 | 0 | 0 |
| | = Earned Ceding Fees | 3,911 | 9,143 | 8,339 | 4,703 | 2,147 | 28,243 |
| - | + *Paid Claims* | *5,606* | *19,799* | *27,614* | *7,695* | *5,737* | *66,451* |
| | - Claim Reserves-BOY | 0 | 3,596 | 5,310 | 2,316 | 686 | 0 |
| | + Claim Reserves-EOY | 3,596 | 5,310 | 2,316 | 686 | 0 | 0 |
| | = Incurred Claims | 9,202 | 21,513 | 24,620 | 6,065 | 5,051 | 66,451 |
| = | + *Amount Due Reinsurer* | *39,960* | *22,470* | *(32,819)* | *(10,062)* | *(6,260)* | *13,289* |
| | + Mortality Reserves-BOY | 0 | 64,733 | 95,584 | 41,680 | 12,346 | 0 |
| | - Mortality Reserves-EOY | 64,733 | 95,584 | 41,680 | 12,346 | 0 | 0 |
| | - Claim Reserves-BOY | 0 | 3,596 | 5,310 | 2,316 | 686 | 0 |
| | + Claim Reserves-EOY | 3,596 | 5,310 | 2,316 | 686 | 0 | 0 |
| | + *Investment Income* | *1,299* | *3,328* | *2,991* | *1,598* | *1,067* | *10,283* |
| | = Statutory Net Income Before Tax | (19,878) | (3,339) | 21,082 | 19,240 | 6,467 | 23,572 |
| | Required Trust Balance | 68,329 | 100,894 | 43,996 | 13,032 | 0 | 0 |
| | EOY Surplus Drain (Gain) | 27,070 | 33,837 | 6,767 | (15,733) | (23,572) | 0 |
| | Total GAAP Income Before Tax | 3,139 | 7,631 | 1,914 | 8,810 | 2,078 | 23,572 |

Figure 5.2. Written reinsurance example

# Chapter Six
# U.S. Regulatory Environment

## OVERVIEW

The insurance industry is one of the most regulated industries in the United States. For the most part, a structure of state regulation has evolved. Most regulation is directed towards the direct writer, but many facets affect reinsurers. Since the scope is broad, this section will only address the aspects that affect producer-owned reinsurers.

Regulations on the direct writer impose conditions which are a major factor in the way reinsurance programs are structured. For business ceded on an earned basis, the direct writer holds the assets, so there are virtually no restrictions on this type of reinsurance. For business ceded on a written basis, the reinsurer owns the assets, so the direct writer imposes significant controls.

If the reinsurer is a U.S. reinsurer, it is subject to the regulations of its state of domicile. Even the most liberal of the state regulatory environments impose significant oversight and costs. Much of the appeal of an offshore reinsurer is the modest regulatory climate.

The U.S. regulatory framework consists of three primary areas of regulation:

- Policy forms and agent licensing
- Statutory annual statements
- Triennial examination process

These regulations apply to all insurance companies domiciled in the U.S. They primarily affect direct writers, but the last two affect U.S. producer-owned reinsurers. Some of the conditions imposed on direct writers affect the way operations are structured with offshore reinsurers. In addition to these general regulations, all states have specific sections which deal directly with credit insurance.

## POLICY FORMS AND AGENT LICENSING

The regulations concerning policy forms are extensive and provide detailed specifications on the form and content of the policies. Credit insurance regulations provide that the benefits must be tied to a specific loan transaction. Combined with the general requirements, this provision has the effect that most credit insurance policies and certificates contain similar provisions.

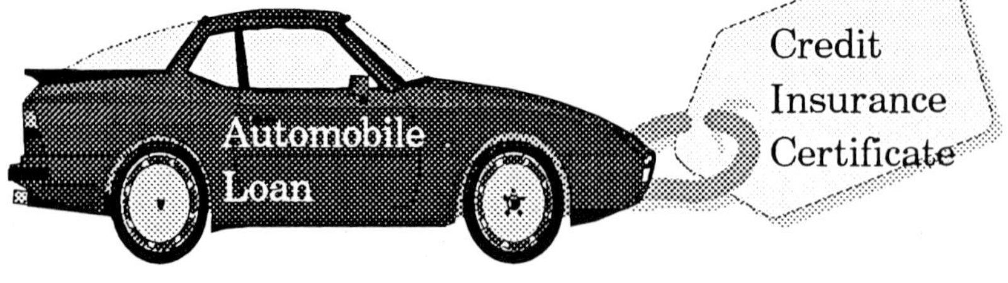


Credit insurance policies must be tied to a specific loan.

Regulations divide life insurance into two categories—individual and group insurance. In ordinary insurance, these concepts are quite different. Under individual insurance, such as a universal life policy, the contractual relationship is between the insurer and the insured. An individual policy is issued as the evidence of insurance. Under group insurance, such as employee group insurance, the contractual relationship is between the insurer and the group policyholder who receives a group policy. Individuals are enrolled in the group and are given a certificate of insurance. The main difference is the level of underwriting conducted by the insurance company. Individual insurance applicants pay different premium rates for the same policy, depending on age, sex, smoking habits, dangerous employment, or unfavorable past medical histories.

Credit insurance is a group concept in that it protects the people in a specified group, e.g., the automobile dealership's customers. There is an indirect agreement between the customer and the insurance company with the dealership as a conduit. Insurance companies issue a group master policy to the automobile dealership. The customers who have loans can obtain this coverage; they are issued certificates of insurance. There is no underwriting comparable to the process for individual insurance. Like other group coverages, one premium rate is charged to all insureds regardless of age, sex or other factors. Some states, however, require the insurance company to issue an individual policy under certain circumstances. While there is a legal distinction, there are no practical differences to the dealership or its customers.

Certain states require that someone at the dealership be licensed as an agent. Each state is different, so general statements are difficult to make. In most states, the group exemption applies—salespeople enroll buyers in the group. They do not have to be licensed as long as they are not directly compensated for the sale. Where licensing is required, most states have a special credit insurance license.

## STATUTORY ANNUAL STATEMENTS

The primary financial control is the requirement that each insurer prepare a financial statement as of December 31, based on **Statutory Accounting Principles (SAP)**. These are rules adopted by the National Association of Insurance Commissioners (NAIC) that place serious restrictions on the operations of U.S. insurance companies.

In contrast to statutory principles are **Generally Accepted Accounting Principles (GAAP)**. GAAP is the usual method of accounting used by all U.S. corporations. The objective of GAAP accounting is to accurately measure net income for the accounting period. This certainly seems reasonable and consistent with the owner's expectations from an accounting system. It answers the question, "How much did we earn last year?"

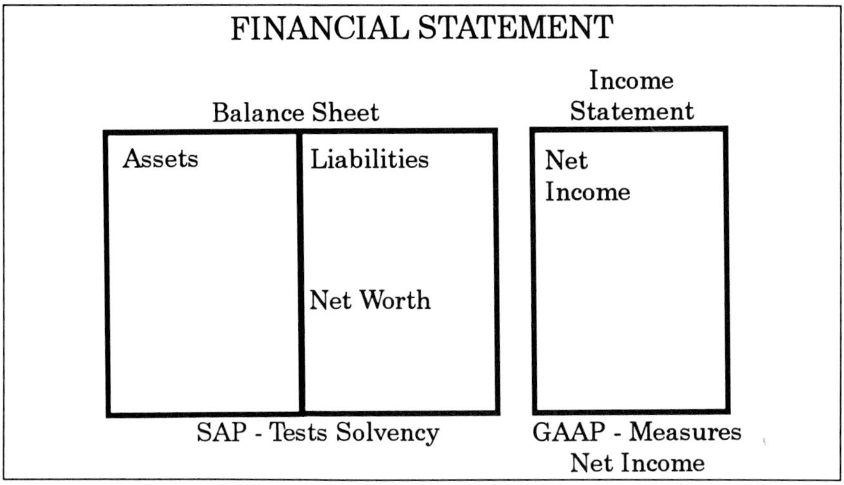


Indeed, the question arises, "Why do we need any other form of accounting?" The contrast between a dealership and an insurer provides the basic answer. Insurance is one of the few industries where income precedes expense. A dealership has "brick and mortar" costs, such as floor planning and parts inventory, before the first car is sold. On the other hand, insurers receive income on day one in the form of premiums, but most of their expenses—claims and administration—occur over the lifetime of the policies. SAP answers the question, "Does the insurer have the financial resources to meet its future obligations?"

Both systems are based on accrual accounting—cash transactions plus accrual items. On the asset side, the accruals include prepaid expenses, accrued interest on invested assets, and amounts due but not received. On the liability side, the accruals include bills unpaid and accrued taxes.

Basic assets and liabilities of the dealership are relatively straightforward to determine. Indeed, it is possible for a dealership to prepare a financial statement within a few days after the close of the year.

These same items apply to insurers but with two important distinctions—the magnitude of the assets and the uncertainty of the liabilities. Insurers collect huge sums of money from insureds and make the promise to provide benefits in the future. In order to protect the insureds, the regulators must be certain that the assets are sound and properly valued, and that the liabilities are conservatively estimated. The liabilities of a dealership are easily determined and measured. Contrast this with the promise to pay a death benefit to anyone who dies out of a group of a million insureds. Or try to predict the amount of future claim payments on a group of 50,000 disabled lives. While the task is daunting at times, the estimates must be made; and the regulators must be satisfied that the estimates are reasonable.

Naturally, an accounting system designed to protect insureds has only one thought in mind—conservatism. Conservatism pervades statutory accounting. It is a test of solvency. The general principle is that if an insurer has a positive net worth after assets are under-valued and liabilities over-valued, then the regulator can feel comfortable that the insurer will be around to meet its obligations.

There are two primary areas where statutory accounting affects credit insurers—commissions and reserves. Consider a disability policy. A single premium is charged for 48 months of coverage. Both SAP and GAAP require that the full premium be established as the reserve on the day of issue, a **gross unearned premium reserve**. At issue, none of the insurance premium has been earned; it is all unearned. The concept is that the premium will be earned as the term of the insurance progresses.

At the same time, a front commission is paid to the dealership at issue. This is an out-of-pocket cash payment. With a 40% front commission, the insurer receives only $60 on a $100 gross premium. **For statutory accounting, all expenses must be charged to earnings on the day they are paid.** The insurer "loses" money the day the policy is issued. It receives only $60 in assets, but must establish a liability for $100. The result is a loss of net income equal to $40. This $40 loss is called **surplus drain**. But this is a temporary loss created by charging expenses as they are paid, while earning the premiums over the term of the insurance. Over time, this temporary loss is recovered along with any real profits.

GAAP accounting corrects this oddity by establishing an asset for the commissions paid—the **deferred acquisition cost** or **unamortized acquisition expense**. At issue, the $100 liability is exactly offset by assets of cash equal to $60 and a deferred acquisition cost of $40. The front commission is simply a prepaid expense that is charged to earnings over the term of the insurance.

But as far as state regulatory authorities are concerned, SAP is reality. They consider the surplus drain to be a real loss. To absorb these losses, an insurer must have sufficient capital, paid-in surplus, or retained earnings.

## Reserves

The insurer must establish reserves in both statutory and GAAP financial statements. There are two types of reserves, which are the same as the reserves described in earlier chapters.

**Active life reserves** are also called **policy reserves**. These reserves are the estimate of future claims that will happen after the accounting date.

To qualify as a life insurance company for tax purposes, an insurer must calculate life insurance reserves based on a mortality table and an assumed rate of interest—a **mortality reserve**. A mortality reserve is used for life insurance policies for statutory and tax reserves, but for all other purposes, unearned premiums are used.

**Claim reserves** are the liability for future payments on claims that have already happened. The concepts are described in Chapter 4. In most cases, the same claim reserves are used for statutory and GAAP financials.

When the direct writer issues a policy, it collects a single premium. Naturally, it must set aside a portion of this premium for future claims—these are the reserves of the company. If it reinsures the business, it is permitted to reduce its reserves for the appropriate portion of the risk that it has ceded to the reinsurer. Certain conditions must be met for the reduction to be allowed. In general, the direct writer can reduce its reserves if the reinsurer is licensed to do business in the direct writer's state of domicile. This is rarely the case even for a U.S. reinsurer. Most U.S. reinsurers are licensed only in one state, and that state is usually Arizona.

Reserve credit is allowed, however, if the reinsurer places the funds it receives in a **custodial trust account** in a U.S. national bank. A custodial trust document is drawn among the direct writer, the reinsurer, and the bank. It specifies the amounts required in the trust, the type of assets which can be deposited, and the conditions under which the direct writer can claim the trust. Most assets that qualify as admitted assets of an insurance company are permitted in the trust.

An alternative to a trust is a **letter of credit (LOC)**. This document is an unqualified promise by a bank to pay funds to the direct writer on demand. Somewhere in the legal documents will be limitations under which the direct writer can claim the funds. The LOC is said to be a **clean, irrecoverable, evergreen** LOC when it is issued for a specific term which cannot be commuted, and there are no conditions on the bank's obligation to pay. The usual term is twelve months.

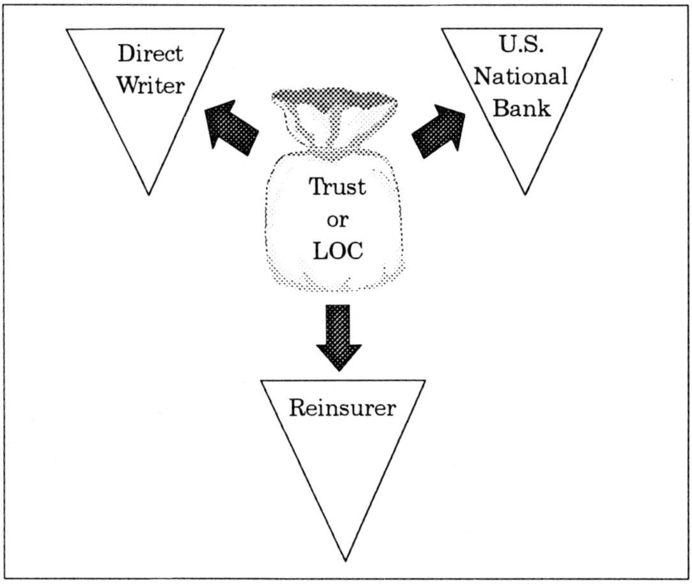

## TRIENNIAL EXAM PROCESS

Every three years, an in-depth review is made of the financial statements of all U.S. domestic life insurance companies. The exam is led by the insurer's state of domicile. The domestic state will schedule the exam, name an examiner-in-charge, and appoint other examiners if needed. If an insurer is licensed in other states, the other states have the right to send examiners also. The trend in recent years is for most examiners to come from the domestic state.

For large direct writers, the triennial exams are a major event. Five to ten examiners may show up and stay for three to six months. It's a major expense and a significant disruption to parts of the organization.

The focus of a triennial exam is on the statutory balance sheet (assets and liabilities) of the insurer. The primary activities are:

| Assets | Liabilities |
|---|---|
| Confirm bank balances | Review reserves |
| Physically inspect ownership documents | Check inforce detail<br>Review actuarial opinions<br>Test claim reserves for adequacy |
| Verify insurer's valuation | Verify unpaid amounts |
| Verify compliance with investment code | Verify calculations |
| Verify calculations | |

If the direct writer reinsures business to producer-owned reinsurers, the examiners will review all reinsurance treaties and custodial trust agreements. The examiners will review the assets in the custodial trusts for both adequacy and quality.

Some review is made of operational areas, but this review is primarily for compliance with state licensing laws and the treatment of policyholders and claimants. All complaints received against the insurer are reviewed for the nature of the complaint and the timeliness and fairness of its resolution. Sample claims may be reviewed for timeliness and fairness of handling.

The general process is similar for a reinsurer, but most steps are less complex. The overall process generally involves only one examiner and less than a month of time. The financial review is nearly identical, but there are few operational reviews, since the reinsurer does not interact with policyholders.

## MARKET CONDUCT EXAMINATIONS

A growing number of states now administer market conduct exams. These exams are directed only at the direct writer, but occasionally will affect the dealership as a producer of business.

Market conduct exams are detailed reviews of insurer and producer compliance with agent licensing requirements, policy form approvals, premium rate calculations and claim handling. On the sale side, the examiner will select a sample of policies that have been sold. The examiner checks that each policy was sold by a properly licensed entity using an approved policy form, and that the rate calculation was accurate and in conformance with the rates that were filed and approved.

On the claim side, the examiner will review denials in particular but will also review a sampling of paid claims.

# Chapter Seven
# The Arizona Reinsurer

## OVERVIEW

The decision to form a United States reinsurer hinges on a desire for a more substantial reinsurer and a more familiar regulatory environment than most offshore programs. These positives are offset by a substantial capital requirement and significant regulatory oversight and constraints.

Within the United States, a number of states have adopted regulations favorable to the formation and operation of reinsurers. Several states—Colorado, Hawaii, Vermont, and others—have clearly encouraged reinsurance companies in recent years. Still, for credit insurance reinsurers, the clear choice is Arizona.

In the 1950s, several early credit insurance reinsurers were formed in Arizona because of low capital requirements—originally $25,000 of paid-in capital and $12,500 of paid-in surplus. The regulatory climate was as relaxed as any state. The number of Arizona reinsurers grew, and gradually the Phoenix area attracted lawyers and actuaries who specialized in the formation and operation of reinsurers. When the door was opened in 1970 for bank holding companies to own reinsurers, the rush went to Arizona where the expertise and regulatory process were already established.

Capital requirements have increased over the years. Arizona set up a special set of requirements for a **reinsurance company**. Now, the required capital is $100,000 and the minimum paid-in surplus is $50,000. A reinsurance company can only assume business from other companies. It cannot issue policies without meeting the higher capital and surplus required of a direct writer ($400,000 and $200,000 respectively). Another popular state is Texas which only required $400,000 until recently.

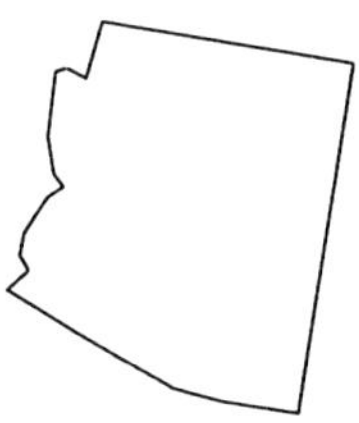

ARIZONA

- $100,000 required capital
- $50,000 paid-in surplus
- Formation in six months
- About $5,000 in formation costs

TEXAS

- $700,000 required capital
- $700,000 paid-in surplus
- Formation in 12 months
- About $20,000 in formation costs

## FORMATION

Formation of an Arizona reinsurer can be accomplished in about six months. Several lawyers and actuaries in the Phoenix area are proficient in the formation process. In addition, the Arizona Insurance Department is well organized and experienced in processing applications.

Formation costs are usually around $5,000. In other states, a formation often takes a year or more and requires significant legal assistance.

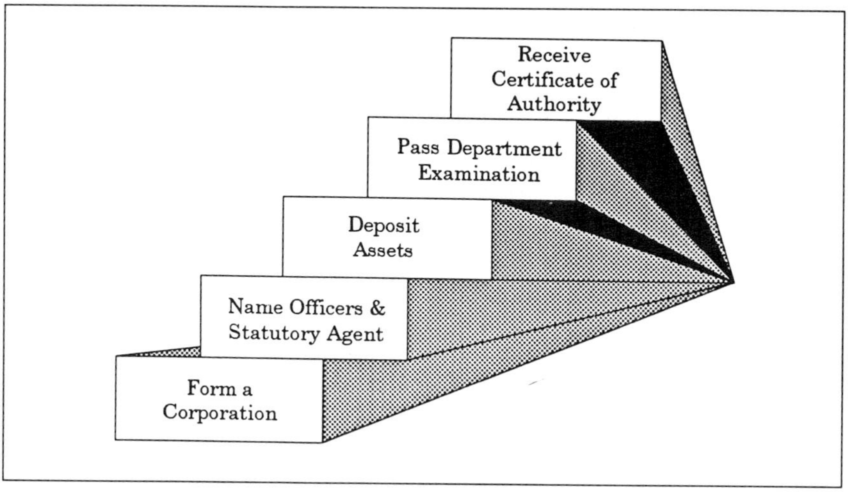


The process begins by selecting a name for the company. The Insurance Department must certify that the proposed name does not conflict with the name of any existing insurance company. Then, an Arizona corporation is formed following the same steps required of all corporations. Three of the five original incorporators must be Arizona residents, but the requirements can be fulfilled by employees of the firm assisting in the incorporation. The incorporators do not have any liability, and once the incorporation process is finished, their role is completed. Articles of Incorporation and By-laws must be written and published in local newspapers. After publication, the incorporation process is completed with some minor paperwork. This stage costs about $300 in publication costs, state fees, and legal fees.

Following incorporation, the company must be licensed as an insurance company. An application to the

Insurance Department is completed, along with several supplementary documents. A biographical form specified by the National Association of Insurance Commissioners must be completed by each member of the Board of Directors and each officer.

An Arizona resident must be appointed as the statutory agent of the company. This is a continuing requirement that is usually fulfilled by the firm handling the incorporation. However, the only requirement to be a statutory agent is that the individual is a resident of Arizona and has been a resident for three years. Most people serving as statutory agents charge $50 per month for the service. This fee may include some consultation on routine matters before additional charges are incurred.

At least $100,000 of the original capital must be placed on deposit with the state. The only valid assets for this deposit are a certificate of deposit issued by an Arizona bank, U.S. Treasury bills, or bonds issued by an Arizona governmental agency. If the market value of the deposit can fluctuate, as with long-term bonds, the amount on deposit must exceed the required amount, so that the Department is not required to watch the market values.

Other assets of the company can be held anywhere. The investment code of Arizona for insurance companies is typical of most states. Standard investments, like certificates of deposit, Treasury, municipal and corporate bonds, and first and second mortgage loans, are all acceptable. Common and preferred stocks are also acceptable.

The investment code places certain restrictions on the percentage of assets invested in any one corporation's stock or bonds, along with general limitations on the percentage invested in common stock. Common stocks cannot exceed 20% of total assets.

As with all states, Arizona requires that certain assets be **non-admitted assets** for statutory accounting purposes. While the reinsurer is permitted to make the investment, it is not permitted to carry the asset on its books in calculating its net worth in the statutory annual statement.

This practice goes back to the early 1900s when rigid rules were established to cure some abusive investment practices of the day. These restrictions have continued and are a fundamental difference between statutory and GAAP accounting. The primary assets that are non-admitted are:

- Loans to officers and directors

- Furniture and equipment, including company cars and airplanes

- Front commissions, ceding fees, and premium taxes that would normally be set up as prepaid expenses

- Other prepaid expenses, including federal income tax recoveries

Reinsurers are permitted to have up to 10% of their assets included as admitted assets if the investments fall into the **basket clause**. These are investments that are neither clearly permitted nor prohibited, but any one investment cannot exceed 2% of total assets.

Aside from the statutory deposit, all assets and records can be maintained outside the state. It is necessary to set up a checking account to handle routine cash transactions. This can be a regular bank account or a money market fund which has check-writing privileges. If the money market fund is operated by a non-bank institution, such as Shearson Lehman Hutton, the account is considered a common stock. The only effect of this classification is that the size of the account is subject to the 10% limitation on investments in any one common stock.

After the initial paperwork is complete, the statutory deposit is in place, and the surplus is contributed, the final step is the completion of a pre-admittance examination by the Department. This takes only a few days of examination time but may take several weeks to schedule. Once the Report of Examination is submitted to the Department, a **Certificate of Authority** is issued, and business can commence.

The reinsurer can now execute a reinsurance treaty and trust agreement with the direct writer and the bank serving as trustee. Once completed, these documents must be submitted to the Department for approval. Since the direct writer will likely be using standard, boiler-plate documents, approval is usually routine.

## ONGOING OPERATIONS

In all likelihood, the operations will be straightforward. Each accounting period, the direct writer will provide a **cession**. This accounting report will specify the cash transactions for the period. A detailed policy-by-policy report may be provided on each issue and refund. A detailed claim report will usually be provided.

Elements of a Cession Statement

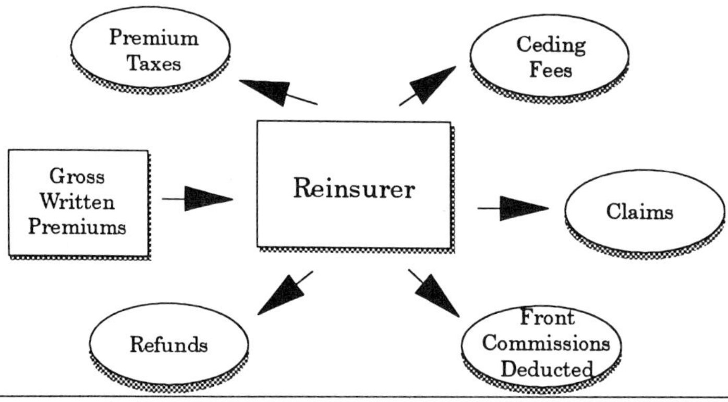


For business ceded on a written basis, a check for the net balance will be sent if the balance is positive. In the first year or two, this will generally be the case, due to the single premium structure of the business. Unfortunately, this cash is not profit. Amounts must be set aside for future claims. Because of statutory accounting rules, the amounts to be set aside can equal <u>or even exceed</u> the cash remitted by the direct writer.

Included in the periodic cession will be a statement of the required reserves which must be placed in the trust account. The reserves are policy reserves (for future claims) and claim reserves (for future payments on claims that have already occurred).

## Year-end Activities

All insurance companies are required to use a December 31 fiscal year. Soon after the end of the year, work on the annual statement begins. For an Arizona-only reinsurer, the statement does not have to be submitted until March 31. All other states require that the statement be filed before March 1.

The reinsurer must also file a Federal Income Tax return on Form 1120L if the reinsurer qualifies as a life insurance company. Otherwise, an 1120-PC (property and casualty insurance company) is filed, unless the insurer qualifies as a tax-exempt non-life company (see Chapter 9), in which case a Form 990 is filed. The regular filing date is March 15, but an automatic extension is available until September 15 if Form 7004 is filed before March 15. For a tax-exempt non-life company, Form 2758 must be filed before May 15 in order to obtain an extension until July 15, and IRS approval is required. Initial calculations must be made, however, since a penalty is imposed on any tax not paid on or before the regular deadline.

Beginning with the December 31, 1991 financial statements, insurers with more than $1,000,000 in annual premiums must have their statutory statements audited by a Certified Public Accountant. A fairly routine exemption from this requirement can be obtained if premium volume is under $5,000,000. If required, the audit can easily add $5,000-$10,000 to the annual cost of operations.

## Triennial Examinations

Every three years, the Arizona Department will conduct a thorough review of the financial statements and operations of each reinsurer. The exam generally takes two to four weeks and is conducted by an examiner assigned by the Department. The reinsurer can specify the site of the exam, which can be held in the offices of the Arizona statutory agent, the offices of the direct writer, or elsewhere. If the exam is held outside of Phoenix, the reinsurer must pay travel expenses and per diem expenses for the examiner.

In all situations, the reinsurer must pay for the cost of the exam. The per-day charges are about $250. Total costs generally run from $4,000 to $7,000.

The examiner focuses on the latest balance sheet (assets and liabilities) prepared on a statutory basis. Assets are reviewed carefully. First, the examiner inspects the original documents, such as bond and stock certificates. Bank confirmations are required on all depository arrangements. A careful review is made for compliance with the investment code.

The examiner reviews the liabilities carefully. When the policy reserves are supported by a detail inforce run from the direct writer along with the proper actuarial opinion, the review is routine. It is common practice to do a more extensive review of the claim reserves. The reinsurer (or its direct writer) must prepare a report showing the paid claims between January 1 and the exam date to verify that the claim reserves held at the prior December 31 were adequate.

Other liabilities are reviewed but are generally small, such as outstanding expenses and accrued taxes. The amount of capital and surplus is then compared to the minimum requirements.

Some review is made of the operations, but this mainly consists of documenting ownership and general activities. Stockholder and Board of Directors meeting minutes are reviewed along with any changes in the list of stockholders, board of directors, and officers.

The examiner prepares a report of examination which includes a summary page documenting any material differences the examiner found with the statutory statement as it was originally prepared. The report notes any aspect of the operations which is not in compliance with the insurance code. Generally, the reinsurer is given an opportunity to discuss these items with the examiner as the exam is in progress to assure that the examiner has correctly interpreted material and to verify the accuracy of the material presented to the examiner. When the examiner's report is completed, an exit interview is held so that the reinsurer is aware of the findings.

The examiner's report is submitted to the Department for a final review. Some items may be discussed between the Department and the reinsurer, but in most cases this stage is an internal review. After the review, the report is filed by the Department, and the official copy sent to the reinsurer.

The reinsurer has 10 days to object before the report becomes public record. For changes in the financial position, it must accept the change or present data substantiating its original values. If any irregularities in its operation or investments are noted, the reinsurer must submit a plan to bring the activity into compliance. In the event of a significant disagreement, the reinsurer has the right to request a hearing to resolve the issue.

## Limitations on Operations

Aside from the financial constraints imposed by statutory accounting and investment restrictions, there are

**Cost of Operation Summary**
**(Amounts Are Approximations)**

| | |
|---|---|
| **Formation** | |
| Required filings, fees | $300 - 500 |
| Legal assistance | $2,000 - 4,000 |
| Initial examination | $1,000 - 2,000 |
| | $3,300 - $6,500 |
| **Annual Costs** | |
| Statutory agent | $ 600 |
| Renewal license fee* | 2, 325 |
| Annual statement filing fee | 155 |
| Accounting costs** | |
| General ledger | $ 1,200 |
| Monthly financial statements | 3,600 |
| Statutory annual statement | 2,500 |
| Federal income tax return | 1,500 |
| Total | $11,880 |
| CPA audit (if required) | $5,000 - $10,000 |
| **Triennial Costs** | |
| Triennial exams | $4,000 - $7,000 |

* Subject to additional assessments
** Some direct writers provide these services and include the cost in the ceding fees.

only a few business constraints. Still, these constraints may be significant if they come into play.

As with most states, the maximum amount of risk that can be accepted on any one life is equal to 10% of the capital and surplus at the prior year end. For example, if the capital and surplus is $150,000, only $15,000 of life insurance can be assumed on any one life. The amount of disability insurance in force is equal to the monthly benefit times the remaining term. Appropriate arrangements must be made with the direct writer or an independent reinsurer if this limitation comes into play. Given the increasing cost of vehicles and extended terms of loans, the total of payments for even some entry-level cars can exceed $15,000. The burden created by this restriction will only increase over time.

A significant sticking point is the limitation on stockholder dividends. Stockholder dividends in any year cannot exceed the lesser of:

- Prior year's statutory gain from operations, or
- 10% of prior year's capital and surplus

Considering that statutory accounting may produce "losses" for a number of years, the committed capital and expected earnings must be considered long-term investments. While the regulations do permit exceptional dividends at the Commissioner's discretion, this restriction can be a real problem when funds are needed more quickly than 30 days.

## STRUCTURE OF COINSURANCE

For a reinsurer with more than $1,200,000 of annual premium income, the usual desire is to be taxed as a life insurance company. To qualify, the reinsurer must have more than 50% of the total reserves in life insurance reserves. For most reinsurers, disability reserves exceed life insurance reserves, so a portion of the disability business must be assumed on an earned basis (where the direct writer holds the reserves).

Depending on the amount of capital and surplus, the overriding concern is the amount of surplus drain that can be absorbed. To accept business on a written basis usually means that surplus must be contributed to the company in excess of the required minimum. The greater the proportion assumed on a written basis, the greater the cash that must be placed in the required trust account. An alternative to lessen the amount of surplus drain is to reduce front commissions.

It is common to begin a reinsurance program with a modest percentage of the life business on a written basis. The remaining life business and the disability business are assumed on an earned basis. As profits emerge, the proportion assumed on a written basis can be increased.

The direct writer will work with the dealership to structure the optimum arrangement. It is critical that the professionals preparing the financial statements and tax returns monitor the structure to avoid unpleasant tax consequences or sudden calls for cash infusions.

## EXOTICS

An unusual ownership structure evolved in Arizona to meet the demands of producer-owned reinsurance. The

desire was for a structure that permitted dealers to participate in a reinsurance program that required limited capital contributions and a spread of the annual overhead cost of operation. The result became known as an **exotic reinsurance company**.

An exotic reinsurer is structured with different classes of stock. In one form or another, the dealership purchases a class of stock, usually for a modest amount ranging from $100 to $10,000. Over time, the value of this stock is directly related to the profits generated by the credit insurance sold by the dealership.

A variety of structures are in place. The following example is a description of one exotic that is typical of the operational aspects of most exotics. The actual details of a proposed plan of operation will be described in an Offering Prospectus, which is often 30-50 pages in length.

Exotic Life was formed by a direct writer (DW) of credit insurance. DW owns 100% of the Class A voting shares. The Class A shares cost $150,000 and serve to provide the required capital and paid-in surplus. All investment income on the capital and surplus inures to the benefit of the Class A shares. Non-voting Class B shares are authorized to be issued as 100 individual series of stock. Each series has a price of $1,000.

DW's sales staff then begins to market the program. When a dealer enrolls in the program, he purchases a series of Class B stock for $1,000. DW then begins to reinsure the business produced by that dealer into Exotic Life and to maintain the loss experience for each series of stock separately. As a part of its ceding fee, DW will perform the usual accounting requirements and handle all procedures with regulatory authorities. It will also be responsible for optimizing the reinsurance on a written/earned split and for filing tax returns.

In general, the profits from each dealer's business benefit his series of stock, but there are some pooling requirements. Investments are usually not segregated by series of stock. All assets are in a general fund. The overall investment performance is allocated by DW to each series in approximate proportion to the assets contributed by each series. In most cases, this allocation is comparable to the earnings if individual accounts had been maintained. The primary drawback (or advantage in some cases) is that DW is making the investment decisions and allocations.

The real negative concerning exotics is the sharing of the downside among the profitable classes. When every series is profitable, the setup works just fine. Problems arise when a dealer goes out of business or a series has poor loss experience. In most cases, DW is unwilling to absorb these losses. DW sets its ceding fee to cover the cost of operation and profit, but a ceding fee sufficient to cover a losing series is so high that dealers will not enter the program.

If a dealer goes out of business, it may fail to remit premiums for business that was sold, or not be there to fund return commissions on refunds. Also, some series take too much front compensation or just have an exceptional number of claims. When a series runs off in a negative position, the loss is allocated among all of the profitable accounts. This is a natural consequence of risk pooling. A good case in point is a recent proposal from a large, factory-promoted exotic offering profitable dealers pennies on the dollar to offset losses on unprofitable dealers.

As with other reinsurance programs, this is a long-term investment vehicle. There are set procedures for selling back a series of stock or withdrawing profits, and most exotics have very conservative rules for these calculations and procedures. Profits from business on repurchased series of stock often benefit the other classes and serve to offset a series that runs off negative. Premature withdrawal from an exotic usually leaves a substantial amount of **MONEY ON THE TABLE**. Plan to stay for the long haul before entering such an arrangement.

Some sophisticated tax planning should be undertaken when using the exotic company structure to enjoy reinsurance earnings. The tax planner should review the tax treatment from the dealership owning a preference share interest in an exotic reinsurance company.

"In one of the few tax decisions dealing with credit life (sic) companies is Liston Zander [see Zander v Comm., 173F.2d 624 (5th Cir. 1949)]. In this case a credit finance company bought a group credit life and accident and health policy covering its debtors. In addition the company acquired a special class of preferred stock from the life insurance company writing the credit insurance. The preferred stock provided for payment of fixed dividends and special dividends based upon profitability of the credit insurance. The court held that since the life insurance company segregated in its financial statements the earnings allocated to the preferred stock for purposes of paying special dividends, these earnings were, in substance, return premiums.

"Accordingly, to maximize tax deferral, the earnings must remain those of the [exotic reinsurance] company, unfettered and available for utilization in operations against potential future losses of any shareholder's business, until distributed."[1]

---

1 Duer, Walter. Captive Insurance Update, KPMG Peat Marwick.

# Chapter Eight
# The Nevis Island Reinsurer

## OFFSHORE REINSURANCE

A number of sites are available for offshore reinsurance, but Nevis Island has emerged as the site of choice for most offshore automobile dealer reinsurers concerned with ease of formation, low cost and reasonable operations requirements. About one thousand insurers are now domiciled in Nevis Island.

The selection of a site for an offshore reinsurance company is made based on three important advantages:

- Formation can usually be accomplished in a matter of weeks, even days if necessary.
- The cost of operation is modest when compared with other sites.
- Procedures are streamlined and regulatory oversight is appropriate for dealer-owned reinsurers.

Tax advantages are not the reason an offshore site is selected. Virtually all dealer-owned reinsurers elect to be taxed in the same manner as a U.S. corporation, consequently they are subject to the same taxation rules as a U.S. domiciled reinsurer.

## SELECTION CRITERIA FOR AN OFFSHORE SITE

Once a decision is made to establish an offshore reinsurance company, there is literally a world of possibilities. Europe and Asia have well-developed insurance markets with locations such as the Channel islands that provide convenient sites for a reinsurance operation. The Caribbean islands have comparable reinsurance facilities and offer the advantages of the use of English and reasonable proximity to the United States.

### Security of Assets

The primary consideration is a location where there is no risk of asset expropriation. Some jurisdictions require that all or a portion of the insurer's assets be deposited "in-country." Most of the Caribbean islands are stable. However, the potential for unrest always exists. Any site not allowing all assets to be held in the U.S. should be eliminated from consideration.

### Minimum Capital Requirements

Given the risks assumed by a dealer-owned reinsurer, high capital and surplus requirements are not necessary. The more established Caribbean sites, such as Bermuda and the Cayman Islands, have requirements that exceed domestic sites ($300,000 and up).

## Regulatory Environment

Some sites have cumbersome restrictions on investments or stiff reporting requirements. The direct writer is in the best position to impose the constraints needed for its protection. Further protection through government regulation is unnecessary.

## Minimal Financial Reporting

While no Caribbean island requires statutory-type accounting, a number of sites require CPA-audited financial statements based on GAAP accounting. In most cases, the audit must be performed by local accountants and is intended to stimulate the local economy. When considering a site ask: Does the country require any financial reporting? If so, what level is required, and does it serve any useful purpose to compensate the reinsurer for the additional cost involved?

Knowledgeable insurance professionals recognize that thorough regulation of an insurance company operation, if necessary to protect insureds, requires expensive audited financial statements. Small island nations are not equipped to impose and oversee these type of regulations. Any regulation other than registering a corporation, maintaining a list, and cashing checks is regulatory make-work.

## Defined Insurance Regulations and Infrastructure

If the jurisdiction has adopted a regulatory infrastructure, separate provisions are needed for dealer-owned reinsurance company operations. These provisions should recognize the built-in regulatory security afforded by the direct writer to the consumer and that imposition of an additional layer of regulations merely costs the reinsurer and does not add to the security of the insured.

The following features ease the conduct of business in an offshore location.

## English Language and U.S. Currency

English is a necessity, and the ability to deal with U.S. currency is helpful. Most Caribbean islands have local currency, but U.S. dollars are the de facto currency. Some countries require that all reporting, including stockholder and director minutes, be translated into the local language. This is an unnecessary expense.

## Minimum Stockholders is One

While it may seem desirable to have a number of stockholders, the preference is often for a single stockholder. Many dealers are making estate plans using various instruments, such as trusts. Ownership of a reinsurance company by a trust or other legal entity may be desirable. Most modern corporate laws have provisions for single shareholder and single director-styled companies. The reinsurer should not be constrained by regulations to have more than one shareholder.

## Annual Meeting Location

Most of these sites are wonderful to visit—once or even occasionally. The requirement for annual "in-country" meetings loses its glamour quickly. Over time, it becomes a significant expense.

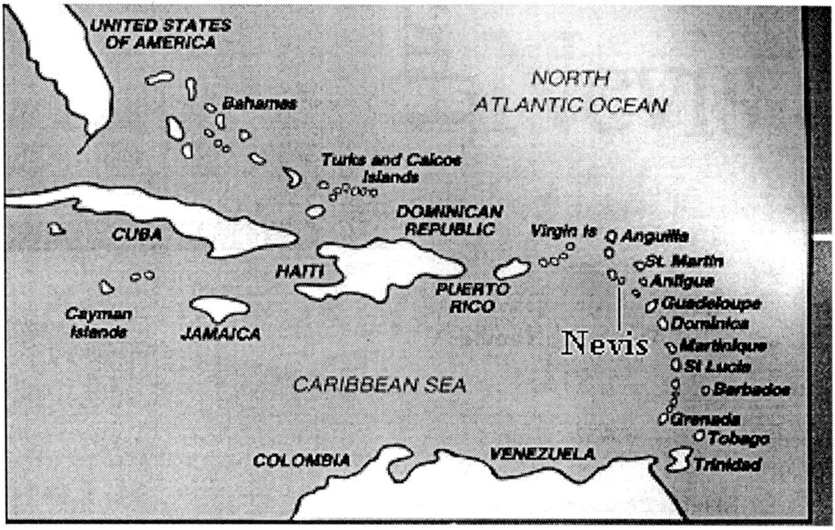


## NEVIS ISLAND

No offshore site so closely matches these criteria as Nevis Island. Other country of domicile possibilities are discussed later.

Nevis is an island of charm and tranquillity. Three thousand foot tall Nevis Peak towers over the 36 square mile island. Lush tropical rain forests cover the mountain slopes where the Vervet green monkey dwells in the surrounding mango trees. The island is located in the northern portion of the Leeward Islands in the Eastern Caribbean, 19 degrees north of the equator. The average temperature is 79 degrees with low humidity. Nevis Island is cooled by northeast trade winds.

Nevis has a rich history with some surprising ties to U.S. history. Alexander Hamilton, a founding father of the United States and the first Secretary of the Treasury, was born on Nevis.

His birthplace now houses the Museum of History and the Nevis House of Assembly.

In the 1790s France attacked American merchant ships in the West Indies. President Adams dispatched the *U.S.S. Constellation* to patrol the Caribbean. At that time, the American Navy had only three warships and had never won, nor even engaged in, a high seas battle. The *Constellation* fought the French frigate *l'Insurgente* off the coast of Nevis Island. The U.S. Navy's first high seas battle was a victory, and this event marked the beginning of its recognition as an emerging world naval power.

About two hundred years later in late 1994, the pragmatic government of Nevis Island opened its arms to dealer-owned reinsurance companies. Working with the private sector, this small island paved the way for the movement of a thousand existing dealer-owned reinsurance companies. In addition, Nevis became an attractive domicile for new corporations.

Credit for this accomplishment is due largely to the leadership of Premier Amory working closely with the Permanent Secretary of Finance Lawrence and chief Legal Advisor Anderson of Nevis. Government officials took the time to understand the nuances and needs of the industry and then shaped their regulatory structure to meet those requirements. They accepted the idea that the regulatory framework must accommodate protection of the consuming public, but regulations beyond that simple premise do not serve a useful purpose. If the regulatory framework does not serve a useful purpose, it has no place on Nevis Island.

Nevis met all of the selection criteria listed earlier. All assets can be maintained in the United States. There are no minimum capital and surplus requirements. The government exercises modest, but appropriate oversight and waives financial reporting for dealer-owned reinsurers.

English is the primary language, and all transactions can be handled in U.S. dollars. The minimum number of stockholders and directors is one. Annual meetings can be held anywhere, including Nevis.

Finally, Nevis Island is an extraordinary place to visit. While tourist facilities are just beginning to develop, there are a number of resorts. The beaches are clean, spacious and empty. Nevis is home to one of the top ten resort hotels in the world and some of the finest Caribbean golf sites.

The Nevisian people are a particular delight, and the government officials have a strong desire to foster the growth of a responsible and legitimate financial center.

## Formation

A primary requirement to qualify for a dealer-owned reinsurance company is that the corporation accept reinsurance. The integrity of the owners is examined by the private sector, who vouches for the credentials of the dealer/owner. The name of the proposed reinsurer must be reviewed for conflicts with other existing names. As with all corporations, a corporate constitution and operational documents must be prepared in conformity with the Nevis legal system.

Several organizations in the United States have developed proven documentation and models that are acceptable to the government of Nevis. For less than $5,000, a reinsurer can be formed in only a few weeks or even a few days, if necessary.

## Operations

The reinsurer is free to conduct its operations as it sees fit. The Government waives financial reporting requirements for dealer-owned reinsurers. The reinsurer can set up its books and records in the manner it finds appropriate. Investments are constrained only by custodial trust requirements imposed by the direct writer. Annual renewal licensing fees are about $1,000.

## Taxation

The Nevis reinsurer normally elects to be taxed as a U.S. corporation. The insurer files the appropriate tax return with the IRS. Life insurers file Form 1120-L. Most casualty insurance companies file Form 1120-PC or Form 990 for tax-exempt non-life company tax status. The reinsurer also makes the Branch Profits Tax election.

It is possible to avoid U.S. taxation as a foreign company, but the maze of rules and regulations is complex. Given the attractive tax treatment available under U.S. laws, the clear choice is to elect to be a U.S. taxpayer. Only a dealership with foreign ownership should consider otherwise.

The complexity of trying to avoid taxes may cost more than the taxes themselves were the company to accept the U.S. income tax system. To avoid U.S. tax requires that the "mind and management" of the company be offshore. This means that all meetings (shareholders, board of directors, committees, etc.) must be conducted outside the United States. All decisions affecting company operations must be made outside the United States. The slightest mistake (such as using a U.S. telephone or the postal service to give the offshore manager instructions) may be fatal to the position that the reinsurance company is not in a trade or business in the United States.

Having the mind and management offshore usually entails hiring a firm of offshore professionals specializing in insurance company management. This adds substantial management fees to the cost of ownership for conducting all meetings offshore. Also, a U.S. direct writer must withhold excise taxes (a percentage of premium) from payments made to a non-U.S. taxpaying reinsurance company. Finally, there is an extra cost to the direct writer (who will pass this cost along to the reinsurer) for non-deduction of the DAC (Deferred Acquisition Cost) Tax. Once these costs are reviewed and compared with the cost of paying U.S. income taxes, the dealer-owner will usually opt to conduct business as a U.S. taxpayer.

Since federal taxation generally follows statutory accounting in the U.S., Nevis reinsurers file the statutory blank with their tax returns. Since the form is required only for tax purposes, it is not necessary to complete the informational and supplementary pages contained in the blank.

The financial statement and tax return for a Nevis reinsurer could be completed by March 15, but most insurers choose to submit Form 7004 and utilize the automatic extension until September 15. (A Form 990 filer completes Form 2758 by May 15 to gain an extension until July 15.) Overall, there is no distinction between a domestic and an offshore reinsurer relative to taxation.

## Cost of Operation

Several U.S. practitioners offer complete accounting and tax services for $2,000-$3,000 per year. Combined with the renewal fee, the total cost of operation is $4,000 or less.

## Structure of Coinsurance

For an offshore reinsurance company, as with a domestic reinsurer, structural decisions depend on financial resources available to meet custodial trust requirements and tax considerations.

If the reinsurer can post the required reserves in the custodial trust fund (or buy surplus relief reinsurance), a substantial portion of the risk can be assumed on a written basis. The remainder must be assumed on an earned basis. To be taxed as a life insurance company, the proportion of business assumed must have life reserves that are greater than 50% of total reserves.

### Exotics

It is possible to operate an offshore exotic, but there are few reasons to do so. Given the low cost of operation, it rarely makes sense to complicate the ownership structure or the operations. An attractive feature of Nevis Island is the ability to have a single-owner operation.

## OTHER JURISDICTIONS

Other offshore jurisdictions are used for dealer-owned reinsurance companies. These have had varying degrees of success, but usually fall short of the full embrace offered by Nevis Island.

### Barbados

Barbados is an emerging country in the insurance field. It has a unique tax treaty with the United States which allows non-U.S. taxpaying reinsurance companies to escape excise taxes imposed by the United States government. Regulatory oversight is quite rigorous, and the financial reporting requirements are substantial. This would be an acceptable trade-off were the dealer-owned reinsurance companies attempting to avoid U.S. taxation, but they are not. Canadian dealers are just beginning to see the benefits of reinsurance and are currently using the exotic company form of reinsurance. For these Canadian dealers to amalgamate and spread regulatory compliance costs may make sense, because the cost to a single-owner reinsurance company is simply prohibitive in Barbados.

### Bermuda

Bermuda is the primary domicile of choice for captive insurance companies. Since the Bermuda market caters to a different type of business than dealer-owned reinsurance, its financial reporting and solvency requirements are difficult and expensive. The required capital and surplus is approximately $300,000 U.S. dollars. Bermuda also requires specialized annual financial statements be signed by a Bermuda-based or approved accountancy. This additional cost of operation is not offset by any other corporate, legal or regulatory features which would favor selection by dealer-owned reinsurance companies.

## British Virgin Islands

For a few years, the British Virgin Islands (BVI) shared domicile of choice honors with the Turks and Caicos Islands for dealer-owned reinsurance companies. While BVI has not adopted formal insurance regulations, BVI has implemented a number of requirements for new and existing reinsurance companies. Among the requirements are:

- Filing of annual financial results
- Filing of the statutory statement of the direct writer
- Filing and approval of reinsurance treaties and trust agreements
- Names of personal and professional references of the owner (who are contacted)

Nearly all automobile dealers redomesticated their BVI reinsurance companies. The dealers saw the compliance costs increasing, with no corresponding benefit to operations—the regulations served no useful purpose. In late 1995, BVI regulators instituted new capitalization requirements and substantial annual license fees. Presumably, these fees were needed to pay overhead for the insurance regulatory office personnel and infrastructure coupled with a lack of companies over which to spread the cost. At this writing, few dealer-owned reinsurance companies remain in BVI; they simply left for more reasonable jurisdictions.

## Cayman Islands

Prior to 1980, this was a favorable jurisdiction for dealer-owned reinsurance companies. However, the country decided to compete directly with Bermuda for captive reinsurance business. The Cayman Islands implemented an attractive insurance framework for the captive business, but it was so broad in scope as to scare away dealer-owned reinsurance companies. Indeed, it was this flight from oppressive regulation in Cayman that jump-started the dealer-owner reinsurance company market.

Cayman requires minimum capital and surplus of $360,000 (U.S. dollars). The Cayman Islands support their regulatory staff by imposing stiff licensing fees for insurance companies. All of this detracts from the attractiveness of Cayman as a site for dealer-owned reinsurance companies.

## Turks and Caicos Islands

For 15 years these islands were the domicile of choice for dealer-owned reinsurance companies. Through a combination of events, this country lost its premier status overnight. One reason the Turks and Caicos Islands (TCI) were abandoned was the disclosure in 1994, by a British Member of Parliament that regulation of all British Dependent Territories in the Caribbean would be "coordinated." TCI regulators have since imposed regulations and costs mirroring the British Virgin Islands regulations.

## Alternative Emerging Nations

Several countries are mentioned as possible new domiciles for dealer-owned reinsurance companies. These countries are being reviewed as alternates to Nevis Island should that country adopt onerous regulations that reverse its current advantages. Countries mentioned most often as alternates are Belize, Nauru, Kiribiti, Tonga and Tuvalu. Indeed, some of the Commonwealth of Independent States (formerly the Soviet Union) may even entertain modern corporate and insurance laws designed to attract dealer-owned reinsurance companies.

Dealer-owned reinsurance is a clean industry for any country. With little rogue activity, its regulatory oversight needs are minimal (that is, cost effective for the government of domicile). Many countries are realizing that dealer-owned reinsurance companies are good corporate citizens and are beginning to design ways to attract them from the current center in Nevis Island.

# Chapter Nine
# Federal Income Taxation

## FRONT COMMISSIONS AND RETROACTIVE COMPENSATION

At least this part is easy. Front commissions and retros are income to the dealership. The dollars received translate directly into taxable income if the dealership is profitable. If the dealership is a regular corporation, this income is taxed at 34%. The income is then subject to personal federal income tax when distributed to stockholders.

If the corporation is a subchapter S corporation, the income is essentially taxed at personal federal income tax rates of 15%-31%, normally at the high end of the bracket. Income is taxed in the year it is earned.

## REINSURANCE

The goal of a reinsurance program is to make more money. Reinsurance offers two sources to earn additional income from insurance activities—underwriting profits and investment earnings. A reinsurance program subjects that additional income to taxation as an insurance company. Few areas of taxation are more complex. Fortunately, for producer-owned reinsurance companies, many of the vagaries and mysteries of insurance company taxation are minimized. In many cases, the tax position is about the same as if these items of income were available at the dealership level (which they are not).

The primary difference between dealership taxation and producer-owned reinsurance company taxation is the timing of when profits emerge from the insurance activity. Commissions are immediate income, while investment income and underwriting profits take much longer to materialize. Few impatient dealers are happy with reinsurance programs. Surprisingly, they prefer to leave **MONEY ON THE TABLE**, rather than wait for profits to emerge from a reinsurance program.

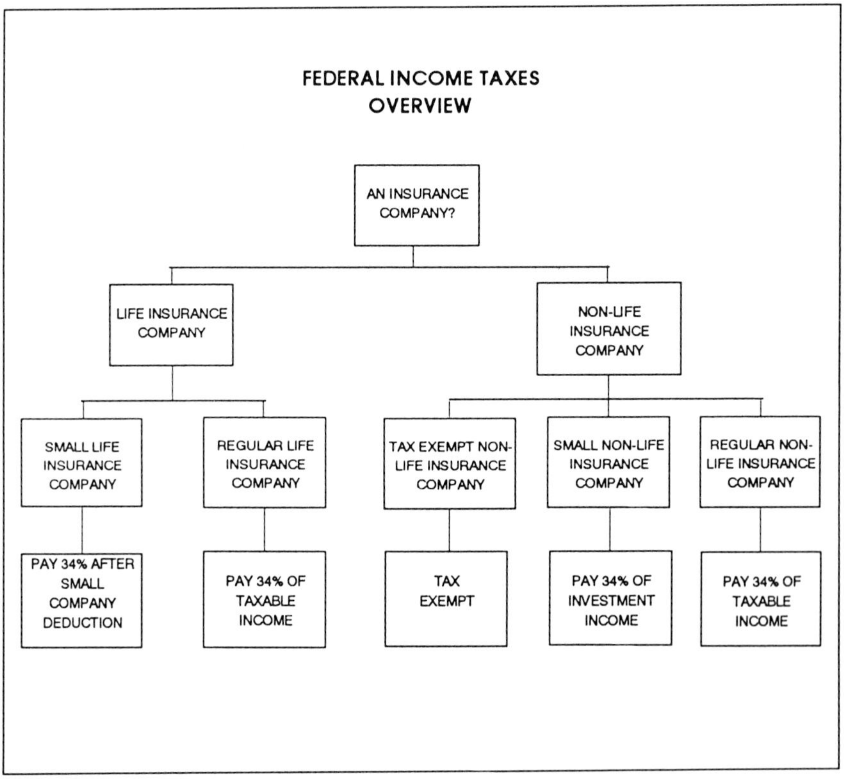

## IS THE CORPORATION AN INSURANCE COMPANY?

From a legal standpoint, a producer-owned reinsurance company is clearly an insurance company, but a test is performed to determine whether it is subject to insurance company taxation under Subpart L of the tax code. This simple test involves the origin of income in the insurance company profit and loss statement. “Is more than 50% of the income from insurance or insurance-related income?” If so, it is an insurance company for tax purposes. *Insurance income* items are premiums. *Insurance-related income* items are items of income that are the result of the insurance activities of the company, such as investment income.

A distinct difference between an insurance company and a general business is that insurance company profits take much longer to materialize. This is a disadvantage to an impatient dealer, but an advantage in overall profitability. The longer it takes for income to emerge, the more investment income can be earned from the deferral of taxation.

The rules for deducting expenses in an insurance company follow Statutory Accounting Principles. Statutory accounting forces the insurance company to immediately expense certain items (commissions, premium taxes, and ceding fees) while Generally Accepted Accounting Principles (GAAP) amortizes those costs over the lifetime of certificates. Secondly, reserve increases are expensed when the certificate of coverage is initially booked.

An insurance company cannot be a subchapter S corporation, so all profits are usually subjected to corporate-level taxation. However, in most situations, producer-owned reinsurance companies will be subject to relatively low levels of taxation because of special treatment for small companies. A reasonable amount of funds can be expensed from the reinsurance company in the form of director fees. The operative word is *reasonable*, as this area can be quite contentious. The IRS' view of reasonableness may be different from the insurance company's view of reasonableness. Any areas such as these must be thoroughly documented and defensible for the insurance company to prevail in any argument about the expense. This is not any different from other expenses that an automobile dealership deducts—be prepared to defend the deduction if the IRS challenges it.

## IS THE INSURANCE COMPANY A LIFE INSURANCE COMPANY?

After determining that the producer-owned reinsurance company is an insurance company for tax purposes, the next test determines whether the company will be treated *for tax purposes* as a life or non-life insurance company.

The test is straightforward for a credit insurance company. The ratio of

$$\frac{\text{Mortality Reserves (on life insurance policies)}}{\text{Total Reserves}}$$

must be greater than 50%. Total reserves are mortality reserves, plus disability unearned premiums, plus service contract unearned premiums, plus disability claim reserves. Why life claim reserves are not in the formula in both the numerator and denominator is a mystery not worth solving.

The amount of disability insurance assumed on a written basis will typically determine whether the reinsurer passes or fails the test. The luxury of having an opportunity in certain cases to select the optimum basis of taxation is a rarity in the tax code, but the issue went to the United States Supreme Court and was resolved in favor of the insurance company taxpayer. [See U.S. v Consumers Life Ins. Co., 97 S.Ct. 1440 (1977)]. Reserves follow the presentation required in the statutory annual statement prescribed by the National Association of Insurance Commissioners (NAIC). For reinsurance ceded on a written basis, the reserves must be shown on the reinsurer's books. Conversely, for the portion of reinsurance ceded on an earned basis, those reserves must be retained on the direct writer's statutory accounting books. Thus, the reserves on an insurer's statutory accounting books are the determining factor in whether a company passes or fails the life insurance company test.

As a side note, the mortality reserves used in this calculation are the reserves shown in the statutory annual statement. As we will see later, these reserves will be greater than or equal to the mortality reserves used to calculate taxable income.

## CATEGORIES OF LIFE INSURANCE COMPANIES

It's not over yet. Having qualified as a life insurance company, the question becomes, "Does the insurer qualify as a small life insurance company?" The good news is that most producer-owned reinsurers qualify. To qualify, the total assets of the controlled group (generally, all corporations under common ownership of 80% or more) must be less than $500,000,000—not a difficult test to pass. To receive the full benefit of being a small life company, the reinsurer must have taxable income of less than $3,000,000. The benefit ceases completely when taxable income exceeds $15,000,000.

Small Life Company Deduction

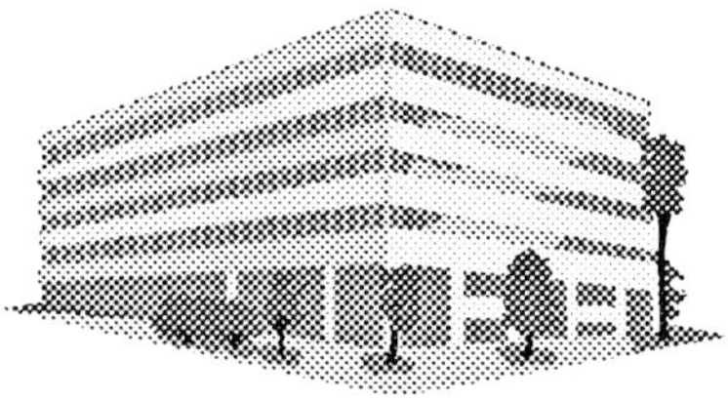

Assets less than $500,000,000 and taxable income less than $3,000,000

Small company deduction equals 60% of taxable income

What is the benefit of being a small life company? The theory of life insurance taxation is that the normal corporate tax rate is applied to taxable income. But a small life insurance company receives a "small company deduction" equal to 60% of taxable income. This effectively lowers the tax rate from 34% to around 17% (once other elements of the tax calculations are included). The deduction begins to phase out when taxable income exceeds $3,000,000 for the year. Few producer-owned reinsurers are in this enviable position.

The primary disadvantage of being a life insurance company is that it is difficult to file consolidated tax returns. This disadvantage is present only when the dealership is a regular corporation. If the dealership is losing money while the reinsurer is profitable, the reinsurer will still pay tax. If the dealership is profitable and the reinsurer has a tax loss, the loss cannot offset the gains unless the reinsurer is a non-life company. There are ways in which consolidated returns could be prepared, but the complexity goes beyond the scope of discussions in this book. Suffice to say, most life companies cannot consolidate with dealerships because of the lack of holding system structures, phase-in time periods, and dissimilar ownership or control.

Small life insurance company profits are subject to about 17% taxation after all prudent expenses. Distribution of dividends to the shareholders then triggers the normal tax for the owner of the reinsurance company. If the capital gains rate is ever reduced below earned income tax rates, the total tax bill could be lower if money is not withdrawn until the company is liquidated.

## CATEGORIES OF NON-LIFE INSURANCE COMPANIES

Failing the 50% life status test means the insurer is taxed as a non-life insurance company. In general, this means being taxed at 34%, but there are also "small" non-life company exemptions that may be advantageous.

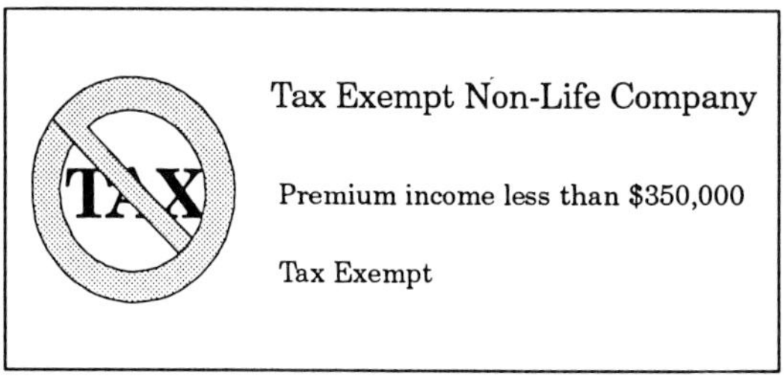


What is a tax-exempt non-life company? If **premium income** is less than $350,000, a special category exists that does not have any formal name. This category is tax-exempt! Needless to say, the IRS is not enamored with this status, but it has processed a number of applications and approved the tax-exempt status. While the Service has vowed to change the status, the law has remained unchanged through several years of technical amendments and tax regulation overhauls.

What is a small non-life company? This is a company that fails the life insurance company test and has premium income between $350,000 and $1,200,000 during the tax year. If the company falls within that category, it can make an irrevocable election to pay full corporate tax rates on the taxable investment income only. There are many things to consider before making this election, including the interplay of alternative minimum taxes and future growth plans for the reinsurance company. Since the election is irrevocable, a great deal of planning should precede the election.

Small Non-Life Company

**Premum income between**
**$350,000 and $1,200,000**
**Option to pay full corporate rate**
**on investment income only**

The interplay among these categories creates uncertainties. For example, does a company lose its *irrevocable* election if the premium income "pops up" beyond the $1,200,000 threshold? What happens if the premium drops back below the $1,200,000 threshold? Does the irrevocable election kick back in? What happens if the company makes the election to be taxed on investment income, then its premium drops below $350,000? Does it now attain tax exempt status? Few taxpayers fall into this corner of taxation, and clear-cut answers to these and other questions have not been developed.

## DIFFERENCES BETWEEN STATUTORY INCOME AND TAXABLE INCOME

In the good old days, statutory income was taxable income. All of the onerous rules of statutory accounting had the pleasant effect of deferring taxes. In recent years, Congress has made several modifications that normally leave taxable income somewhere between statutory income and GAAP income.

### Tax Reserves

**Mortality Reserves**. Reserves must be based on a recognized mortality table and a rate of interest. For statutory purposes, most direct writers use the 1958 CET (or its equivalent, 130% of the 1958 CSO table) or the 1941 CSO Table. In recent years, some insurers have moved to more modern tables like the 1960 CSG, the 1980 CET or the 1980 CSO table. Most states limit the interest rate to 4.5% or less. A 3% rate is still the common industry standard.

A special calculation must be made using the 1958 CET at interest rates specified in tax regulations. The interest rates vary by year of issue and original policy term. Overall, the current rates average about 7.5%. The reserves used to determine taxable income are <u>the</u> <u>smaller</u> <u>of</u> these tax reserves or the reserves used in the statutory annual statement. If both are calculated on the 1958 CET, tax reserves are about 92% of the statutory reserves. If the statutory reserves are on the 1980 CSO or the 1980 CET, these reserves will be less than the 1958 CET, regardless of the interest rates used. In this case, the statutory reserves are the reserves for the calculation of taxable income.

**Disability Unearned Premiums**. The tax calculation for disability policies is addressed as a part of the DAC tax in the following pages.

## Claim Reserves

**Disability**. In calculating claim reserves for statutory and GAAP purposes, the actuary must estimate the total future claim payments on all claims that have already happened. Given a reserve that is established at December 31, about 55% of these payments will be disbursed in the next 12 months and another 30% in the subsequent 12 months. Therefore, the time value of money is a factor but not a major one. As a general rule, if the future disability claim payments are discounted back to the beginning December 31 at 8% interest, the reserves are reduced about 7%. The IRS annually prescribes the minimum interest rate that may be used.

If the statutory reserves are not discounted for interest, an interest discount at federally prescribed rates of interest must be determined and used in the calculation of taxable income. If statutory reserves are discounted, the tax reserves are the lesser of the statutory reserves or the reserves calculated using the tax discount rates.

**Life Insurance**. The same principle is not applied to life claim reserves. Over 75% of the payments associated with the December 31 reserve are disbursed by the following March 31, so any interest discount is trivial.

## The DAC Tax

Clearly the major difference between statutory accounting and GAAP is the immediate expensing of front compensation and premium taxes. Tax rules accepted this treatment prior to 1990. The modification introduced did not require that the actual compensation be amortized; rather, a general formula was developed which only requires a partial amortization. While the procedure became known as the DAC (deferred acquisition cost) tax, it was not a new tax, just a change in the timing of when the taxes were paid.

**Life Insurance**. Each year a set percentage of net written premium must be set up as a capitalized expense. For group insurance the amount capitalized is 2.05% of net written premium for the year. In the few situations where credit life insurance is written on individual policy forms, the capitalization rate is 7.7%.

The expense is amortized over the next ten years on a straight-line basis. One-twentieth is amortized in the current tax year, then nine years at one-tenth, and one-twentieth in the eleventh year. (The tax code permits small life insurance companies to amortize the expense over five years, but the rule does not apply to reinsurance.)

**Disability**. The same concept was implemented somewhat differently for disability insurance. Simply put, an insurance company can deduct only 80% of its disability unearned premiums in calculating taxable income. The method used to calculate unearned premiums in the statutory statement (Rule of 78, pro rata, or mean) is also used to perform the tax calculation.

## Miscellaneous

Any general rules applying to corporations normally apply to insurance companies. For instance, the deduction for meals and entertainment is limited to 80% of the out-of-pocket expense. Normal business expenses are deducted in the same manner as they are for a dealership and require the same standard of reasonableness, especially compensation paid to a controlling shareholder. In addition, the tax rates for taxable income less than $100,000 are lower than the regular rates. Given the taxable income of many producer-owned reinsurers, this facet often lowers the effective tax rate below 17%. The small life company deduction and the elimination of underwriting profit in small non-life companies are considered preferential items of income. These items are added back into income for the alternative minimum tax (AMT).

## THE NEED FOR PROFESSIONAL ADVICE

Insurance company taxation is a specialized subset of general taxation. Competent professional advice is particularly needed when the reinsurance is initially established. Then, a semi-annual review is needed to keep the program on the right track and to recognize opportunities.

## CAVEAT

This chapter is intended to provide a general overview of taxation as it exists in late 1992. It is not intended to provide tax advice. As with any aspect of taxation, the rules are subject to interpretation by the IRS and the courts. A major problem in dealing with taxation is the constant change caused by revisions to the tax code and its implementing regulations. There were four major changes in the statutes in the 1980s affecting insurance company taxation, and more are certain to come.

# Chapter Ten
# The Direct Writer

A wide range of insurers participates in the sale of credit insurance products through automobile dealerships. Since dealerships exist in virtually every city of any size, the marketplace is geographically diverse. The result is that more than 200 insurers participate, using both direct sales forces and general agents. It is estimated that 60% of all installment loans are generated by automobile sales, and the majority of the credit insurance sold on these loans is produced at the dealership level. Except for a few credit insurers that specialize in one market segment, most credit insurers find it desirable to participate in the automobile segment if they want to generate any substantial volume.

Insurers generally can be categorized as:

Full-line ordinary companies

- National
- Regional

Credit insurance specialty companies

- National
- Regional
- Motor Vehicle Manufacturer Insurers

Full-line companies are insurers which offer the entire gamut of life, annuity and health products. Credit insurance is one small segment of a large operation. Often, it is just one segment of the group insurance division. Most of these insurers are national in scope of operations, but fine regional companies also participate.

The general advantage of these companies is the huge asset base they command and their strong financial stability. Offsetting this advantage of financial size is the lack of relative importance that credit insurance may play in the overall corporate picture. The reverse of both also holds. A few large insurers have gotten into financial trouble, and several credit insurance departments of larger insurers provide fine service. A few began as specialty credit insurers and then expanded into other lines.

National specialty companies are often one subsidiary in a corporate family of insurers, so it is difficult to separate them from full-line insurers. In general, they are characterized by a separate corporate identity which specializes in credit insurance or related lines.

Because of the geographic diversity, many regional or even one-state companies write credit insurance. Texas abounds with insurers. Other states fostered the growth of one-state operations with discriminatory premium taxes (particularly Oklahoma). Some widely-licensed operations have one-state subsidiaries for a local presence or to take advantage of premium tax laws.

Profit margins eroded greatly in the 1980s, and the result was a wave of industry consolidations in the last few years. Many one-state and regional insurers got out of the business or were sold to other insurers. Several national operations were sold. This market shake out is expected to continue into the mid-1990s.

Finally, insurers owned by the vehicle manufacturers garnered an increasing market share in the 1980s. The primary insurers in this category are owned by the largest domestic manufacturers—Ford and General Motors. While these insurers were around in 1980, they were not aggressive in the marketplace. Their presence and market share increased in the 1980s because of more aggressive marketing and the increasing reliance on manufacturer financing programs.

Criteria for Selecting a Direct Writer

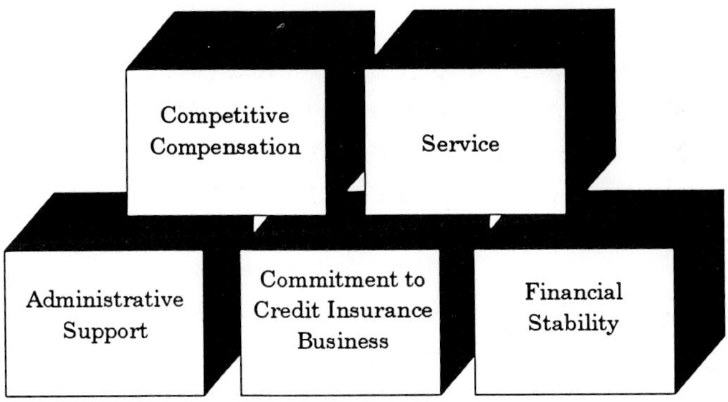


Still, the dealership needs depend only on a limited set of criteria. The primary need is competitive compensation and, preferably, an option to move to more advanced forms of compensation as volume grows. Since this desire is foremost, it is almost a marketplace given. When all of the guaranteed elements of compensation are included, the total compensation packages for most insurers are within a rather narrow range.

The next need is service, and service primarily means training. Higher commission percentages are of little value if the volume of sales is lower. Dealership personnel need good product and sales indoctrination at the outset. Periodic refresher meetings are of great help. The F&I people need occasional reminders of the critical part credit insurance plays in overall profitability. A good system of penetration reports is needed, and the results should be reviewed carefully. Every missed sale leaves **MONEY ON THE TABLE**.

Sometimes insurers charge for the schools or meetings. If an insurer or general agent is putting on a quality show, it's worth the cost. When no charge is made, the cost is being recovered from direct charges or out of money that could otherwise be paid as commission. Is the training provided of good quality? There is only one way to be sure—attend one of the classes. Just a few marginal sales will recover any costs that are involved.

Administrative support by the general agent or insurer is important, but if operations are really smooth, the dealership may barely be aware of the support. If the reaction is "what support?", ask whether the invisibility is because the dealership's needs are being met so smoothly that the support is not even noticed.

Products are relatively standard, but differences do exist. Are all needed products available, e.g., is 7-day retro available (if permitted)? Is underwriting required? Are the policies readable? Credit insurance is a simple product—most of the dealership's customers should be able to understand what the policy says.

Rate calculation materials are important and should be usable and straightforward. The thick rate charts of the 1960s and 1970s have given way to factor cards and hand-held calculators. Factor cards look daunting but can be mastered with a small investment of effort and a good teacher. In untrained hands, the results can be a real mess. This can cost the dealership money. If factor cards are used, verify with the insurer that calculations are being done correctly.

For the reasons above, small printing calculators are widely used. These machines provide much more reliable results. Their use is encouraged even if the dealership must foot the bill.

Larger dealerships have now moved to personal computer-based systems. These systems provide some advantages over hand-held calculators in that loan data is entered only once, and the output is an integrated loan and insurance package.

These wonderful machines do exactly what they are told. The initial programming must be accurate and any reprogramming must be done carefully. The good news is that they will be consistent, if nothing else. An error becomes apparent quickly, but a lot of policies can be issued before the error is found.

The way rate changes are handled is important. In the northeastern states, rate changes are fairly frequent. Pennsylvania requires an annual review of loss experience to determine whether a change is required. Other states require a review every two or three years. Each year, five or so states make changes to prima facie rates.

The process by which rates are changed can be a burden on the direct writer and the dealership. Often, a state will propose a rate change by calling for a hearing. The proposed change will have an effective date 60 to 120 days after the change is adopted. The trouble is that the process is so erratic that one cannot implement the change until the regulation is finally adopted.

Rate changes affect everyone's income and are often hotly contested in the political arena. The hearing is just one aspect of the process. A great deal of lobbying takes place. Positions become polarized. Even after the hearing is complete and the change adopted, the political pressure may continue right up to the implementation date. Because of the intensity, an insurance department may not be in a mood to delay implementation or to make concessions for a smooth change. In the last ten years, there have been situations where rate changes were required on ten days notice.

The bottom line is that insurers who make smooth rate changes are to be valued. Adequate notice of a change should be given, along with clear instructions on the implementation date and procedures. Good direct writers and general agents will keep you, the dealer, informed of rate activities under way in your state. A rate change should not come as a surprise to you. Indeed, your input and support should be solicited, so that the dealership's interests are protected in the process. Get involved—either directly or through the state association. Recognize that the direct writers are not in control. Insurance departments with a limited concept of the impact at the dealership level are making most of the timing decisions.

Financial stability and a commitment to the credit insurance business are other considerations in choosing a direct writer. A change of carriers is certainly a hassle that takes time away from the dealership's primary business of selling cars. A stable, long-term relationship has real value, so an insurer that will be in the marketplace for the long haul is a necessity.

One measure of financial stability is the **Best's rating**. This is a rating assigned by the Best's Insurance Services on an annual basis. Best's reviews the statutory annual statement and may have direct contact with the insurer about its operations. A rating from A++ down to F is assigned.

Any of the "A" ratings by Best's is a sign of financial strength. They are relatively difficult to obtain and are generally limited to the larger insurers. Best's ratings of B and B+ are also indicative of strength.

While the presence of a B rating or higher is assuring, the lack of such a rating is not the end of the world. Many small regional companies are well run and have the necessary financial resources. In addition, the Best's evaluation system often penalizes credit insurers, particularly those active in reinsurance.

If the dealer operates in the more advanced compensation arena by reinsuring business produced in the dealership, the direct writer's Best rating loses some of its importance. The underlying policies are funded in the custodial trust account by the producer-owned reinsurance company. Thus, if the loss ratios are proper, the consumer claims should all be honored regardless of the financial condition of the direct writer. In the early 1980s, a direct writer got into financial difficulties with some of its other product lines. Control of the direct writer was seized by the Department of Insurance. The Department, after evaluation of the assets and liabilities of this insolvent insurance company, determined that claimants would be paid only pennies on the dollar. This would have created serious customer satisfaction problems for the dealerships even though the dealerships had nothing to do with the insurer's impairment. Fortunately, many of the dealers using that direct writer were in producer-owned reinsurance companies. The customers of these dealers received full one-hundred-cent dollars on their claims, because the reserves were fully funded in the custodial trust account.

The same scenario was repeated in the automobile service contract insurance world. Producer-owned reinsurance companies were protected when a direct writer became impaired. One dealer in the Northeast wrote both "walkaway" and reinsured service contract insurance with a now insolvent insurance company. He complained that the "walkaway" service contract insurance was only being honored pennies on the dollar, while the reinsured policies were being honored with full one-hundred-cent dollars. The difference was evident—his reinsurance company had maintained quality assets in the custodial trust account in sufficient amounts to honor the claims. The now impaired direct writer's assets backing up the "walkaway" service contract insurance were diluted in paying all the claimants in the bankruptcy proceeding.

As this book goes to press, one of the factory financing companies has proposed to finance only insurances of companies with "A" ratings. Whether this is a trial balloon or a firm corporate position will remain to be seen. If this tactic is successful, the factory's own insurance companies will benefit, as competition will erode. However, success may be measured with the simple economic concept called "elasticity of demand." If dealers revolt and take financing elsewhere due to factory financing rules, the factory will lose more business than it gains and will soon revisit its proposed change.

A commitment to the credit insurance business, particularly the dealership market, is important. Consider the volume of business written by the insurer. National volume is important, but the market share in a particular state may be just as critical. Ask for market share data. Consider the insurer's years in the business. Talk with friends. Everyone promises good service and personal attention—find out who has delivered on those promises.

# Chapter Eleven
# The Direct Writer's Representative

The dealership is the real customer of a credit insurer. The insurer will attempt to reach its customers through a direct sales force or independent general agents (or sometimes both). Both systems work. Neither system is inherently better—it is the implementation and support of the system by the insurer and the quality of the dealership's particular representative that carry the day.

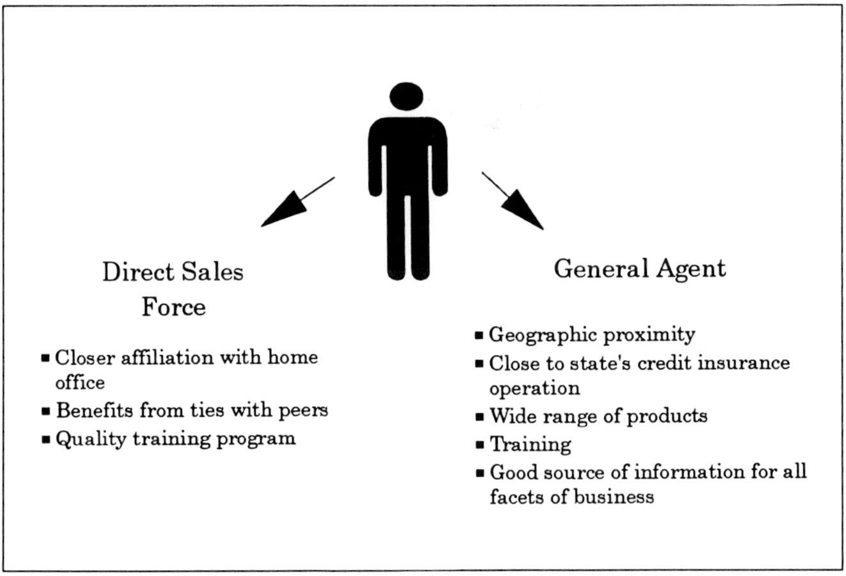

This chapter contains direct statements about the advantages of each system, but the two systems are similar, and such statements do not imply that the same facet of service cannot be performed by the other system.

## The Direct Sales Force

The direct sales force has the advantage of a large support organization to provide services, information and material. Being an employee of the insurer, the representative has a close affiliation with the home office employees. Good field representatives cultivate a relationship with home office personnel as carefully as they entice customers. For the dealership, this means the home office will act quickly to resolve disputes or answer questions.

A direct sales force benefits from association with peers from other parts of the country. Internal sales meetings are an opportunity to hear of approaches or product development in other states. In addition, close contact with home office personnel and company newsletters serve to keep the representative informed and current.

Insurers using a direct sales force usually invest heavily in a quality training program. Indeed, most of these insurers built their business on training. The financial commitment to some of these programs is substantial. In addition, the programs are often conducted by professional trainers hired exclusively to educate in the nuances of finance and insurance.

## The General Agent

Given the geographic diversity of the automobile market segment, many insurers obtain business through general agents. Only a limited number of credit insurers have committed the resources to the widespread direct sales force required to properly service the automobile dealer market segment.

General agents can be categorized as personal producing general agents (PPGAs) or simply GAs. PPGAs are GAs who produce their business directly and do not have any sub-agents. They operate from relatively small offices or from home. They may even be sub-agents for other lines of business. These agents produce from $25,000 to $2,000,000 per year of annual premium.

Once a GA reaches $1,000,000 or more of annual production, he begins to develop a sales staff or cultivate sub-agents. GAs in this category may develop beyond one state into a regional operation. Still, the primary benefit of a GA is local sales and service, so geographic expansion may not be an advantage.

GAs bring several pluses to the table. Their primary advantage is geographic proximity. This is of real value. Service calls may be more frequent. Supplies arrive faster. The dealership can be visited personally if necessary.

In addition to physical closeness, the GA will be close to the operation of credit insurance in his state. Everything that affects the dealership relating to credit insurance directly affects the GA. He is directly interested in the market and the political activities in the state and may even participate in the legislative process. He will have a knowledge of the nuances of business in the state. While credit insurance is relatively consistent from state to state, material differences do exist.

GAs usually represent only one or two credit insurers. Many also provide a wide range of non-credit insurance products from a number of insurers.

Training will usually be provided by the GA. He may have a proprietary program or use one supplied by an insurer. In any event, the physical closeness permits a quick set-up for new employees and the option to have short refresher meetings and seminars. The GA is often involved in recruiting replacement F&I personnel and is better equipped to provide the dealer with vacation/sickness relief at the Finance and Insurance desk.

Most GAs will offer more products than just credit insurance (see Chapter 13). They will likely offer a service contract program and may offer a variety of other products. Some products are for the dealership's customers, but some may be for the dealership, such as group life and health insurance, director's insurance, and garage keeper's liability insurance.

The GA will have economic buying power from the insurer. Since he controls a substantial volume, he is in a position to bargain for the best deals. Insurance programs are his primary business, so he is in a position to negotiate better than the individual dealership. Still, this power may benefit the GA rather than the dealership.

The GA can be a good source of information about products and other facets of the business. He can provide insight about the most profitable disability plan, the value of underwriting, or other issues. He may also know of special products that can be sold. For example, a few states permit dismemberment coverage for an extra charge.

A local representative of an insurer can provide most of these same benefits. The primary question is "How close is the dealership's particular representative?" Some insurers commit to a large direct sales force. Indeed, they provide the same level of service.

A comparison between the amount of front compensation available to the dealership may not show significant differences. On average, GAs receive about 3% of premium for their services. This cost is comparable to the cost of a direct sales force. Certainly there are no blanket statements that can be made comparing one to the other.

Service depends on contact. Geographic proximity is of no value unless the representative actually shows up at the dealership's door. Close doesn't count except for tactical nuclear weapons. Keep track of his visits. Talk to the competition. How many visits can be expected? Again, talk to friends in the business. Which representative has delivered on his promises?

# Chapter Twelve
# Vehicle Service Contracts

Although far different from life and disability insurance, a vehicle service contract (VSC) provides important insurance protection to the consumer and a significant source of potential revenue to the dealership. The wide variety of contractual arrangements and compensation methods presents the dealer with a complex matrix from which to choose.

## THE BASIC COVERAGE

### New Cars

All VSC arrangements share a basic premise of protection against mechanical breakdown of the automobile. The protection that is offered in a VSC supplements the mechanical breakdown protection provided by the manufacturer with each new car sold, the **manufacturer warranty**. The VSC has a term of coverage that normally extends beyond the term of the manufacturer warranty. For that reason, VSCs are often called **extended service contracts**.

The manufacturer warranty always contains a **base period warranty** that is comprehensive and may include a **power-train only (PTO) warranty** on certain major components following the base period. The base period warranty normally applies only during the first 36 months of ownership or 36,000 miles, whichever comes first. This 36 month/36,000 mile (abbreviated 36/36,000) protection is common on most domestic and foreign models. Protection during the base period is usually "bumper-to-bumper." All repairs caused by mechanical breakdown are covered. This excludes normal wear and tear and routine maintenance service.

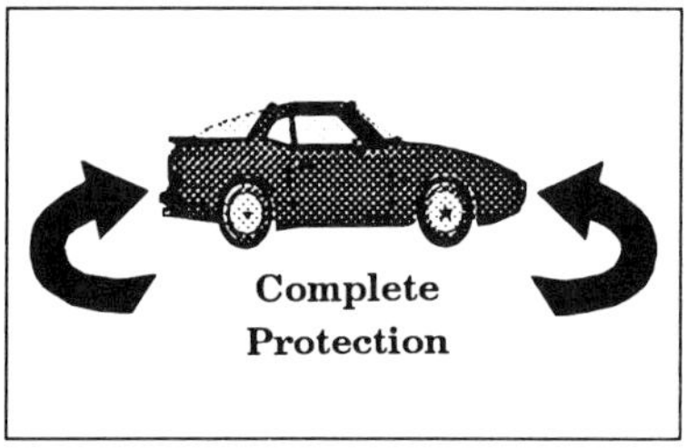


After the base period, some manufacturers provide a warranty on the power-train components for periods up to 72 months/84,000 miles. This warranty protects only the specified components for mechanical breakdown. Repairs are often subject to a deductible.

While this description provides a general picture, the individual variations are numerous. Each manufacturer has its own package and may even vary the package for different models. It is common for a manufacturer to vary the protection by model year to reflect basic sales strategies or to respond to market conditions. Domestic manufacturers provided a base 12/12,000 and a 24/24,000 extended warranty until the mid-1980s when Chrysler upped the ante to 60/50,000 and then 84/70,000 on the PTO warranty to counteract consumer concerns about reliability.

Given the manufacturer warranty, the VSC serves to wrap around the base period warranty and PTO period warranty to maintain near "bumper-to-bumper" coverage. The VSC normally extends the coverage from the end of the manufacturer period until five, six, or seven years.

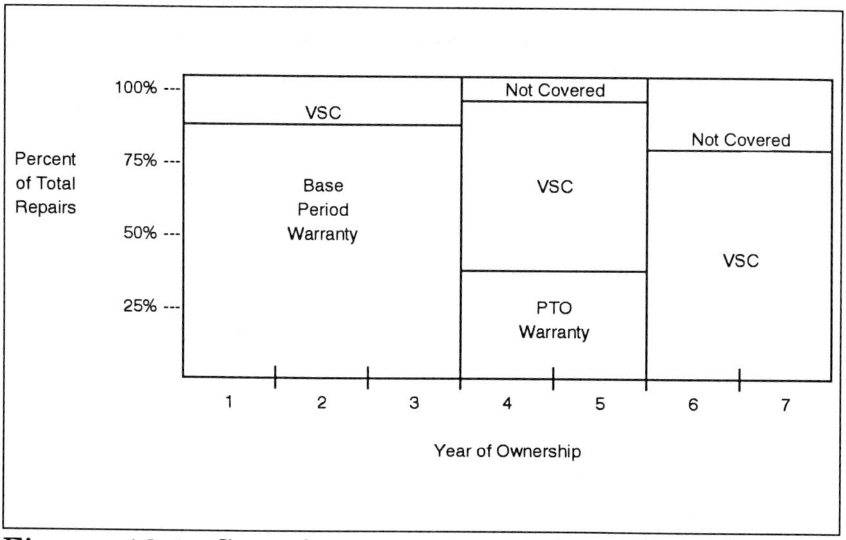


Figure 12.1. Sample percentage of total mechanical breakdown costs covered by various programs.

The VSC provides little benefit during the base period of the manufacturer warranty. However, it may provide benefits for towing, car rental, or payment of a deductible, if such benefits are not included in the manufacturer warranty.

During the PTO warranty period, the VSC covers the mechanical breakdown of most other components excluded from the manufacturer program. It may also cover any manufacturer deductible. Beyond the term of the manufacturer protection, the VSC protects all covered parts until the time or mileage limits of the VSC are reached.

VSC protection is not necessarily "bumper-to-bumper." Most VSC providers offer two or three plans that vary in the extent of coverage. A VSC covers most metal components but may exclude hoses, gaskets and other such parts. Towing and car rental during repairs are often provided, but the benefits vary by type of repair. Membership in an automobile travel club and other services are often included in the top-of-the-line plan. Most programs have deductibles which apply to certain repairs. If the manufacturer offers only a base-period warranty, a basic VSC plan may be available just covering the power-train.

### Used Cars

Similar programs are available for used cars. The protection is somewhat more limited in terms of covered repairs and components. Insurers may also offer a 3 month/3,000 mile coverage that is purchased by the dealership and included in the cost of the automobile. Other protection is sold as an optional cost item to the consumer. This protection is normally sold in 12 months/12,000 mile increments which rarely exceed 36 months/36,000 miles.

## TYPES OF VSC CONTRACTUAL AGREEMENTS

In the current market, the dealership can choose from three basic types of VSC arrangements and a fourth option which shares the same basic coverage but represents a fundamentally different contractual foundation. The difference among the four types relates to the party (the **obligor**) who bears the contractual obligation to the consumer. The four potential obligors are:

- The dealership
- A VSC administrative company
- The manufacturer
- An insurance company

## The Dealership as Obligor

Currently, a large number of programs are designed in which the contractual relationship is between the dealer and the consumer. Here the dealership provides the promise to pay for repairs (or to reimburse the consumer). Repairs must be made at the dealership, except in certain circumstances, such as breakdown more than a specified number of miles away from the dealership.

The dealership has the option to self-administer the program or to contract with an administrative service company, a **third-party administrator (TPA)**. It then must choose whether to self-insure or to purchase insurance protection. The TPA will have an arrangement with an insurer to provide the insurance product—sometimes with an affiliated property and casualty insurer.

Under the arrangement, the dealer is free in most states to set the price charged the consumer. The TPA will charge a flat fee per contract for administration, and an insurer will charge a flat fee per contract for the insurance protection. The charges vary by make and model, new car versus used car, etc. The insurer will often offer two or three programs providing various levels of coverage.

## The TPA as Obligor

Many administrators are set up as service companies and can be named as the obligor in the 16 states where this is permitted. Here the TPA is responsible to the consumer for performance under the contract. The TPA markets the package, which includes administration and insurance for the contractual obligation, to the dealership. The dealership is charged a flat fee per contract, which varies by make, model and other factors.

In most states the dealership can set the retail price charged the consumer. The charge from the TPA is the wholesale cost, and the difference is commission.

Most TPAs purchase an insurance policy for all contracts from one insurer. There are 40-50 large TPAs across the country and an equal number of property and casualty (P&C) insurers providing the underlying insurance product. The TPA may be a subsidiary or affiliated company of the P&C insurer. Each insurer works with a limited number of TPAs or may even have exclusive arrangements.

## The Manufacturer as Obligor

All of the domestic manufacturers and some foreign manufacturers have programs similar to the TPA arrangement. The only difference is that the administrator and insurer are both affiliated with the manufacturer.

While the dealership has some flexibility on pricing, there are more constraints on the retail charge to the consumer. Again, the commission to the dealership is the difference between the retail charge and the cost to the dealership for the administration and the insurance protection.

For new cars, the manufacturer program insures only the makes and models produced by the manufacturer. In the near future, manufacturers are likely to expand in the VSC arena to insure other product lines. On used cars, the manufacturers have programs covering a wide variety of makes and models if the dealer is the obligor.

## The Insurance Company as Obligor

A variation on a VSC is Mechanical Breakdown Insurance (MBI). Here the individual consumer is issued an insurance policy from a property and casualty insurer. The dealership, acting in the role of insurance agent, markets the product to the consumer.

The direct insurance relationship with the consumer imposes substantial constraints on the product, its marketing and its pricing. As an insurance product, the contract constitutes an insurance policy which must be filed with and approved by the Insurance Department of the state in which it is issued. This includes filing of rates. Once filed, the rates become the retail price to the consumer with no room for dealer variation. The insurer will set the commission as a percentage of premium.

To market the product, at least one individual in the dealership must obtain a full property and casualty insurance license. This requires a commitment of time for study and the successful completion of a state examination. There are a number of requirements for continuing education in many states.

From the standpoint of the protection provided, MBI policies are comparable to a VSC. Because of the regulatory constraints, MBI represents a very small portion of the VSC market. Less than 5% of the VSC market is insured through this product line.

## Summary of Options

| Obligor | Administrator | Insurer | Contract |
|---|---|---|---|
| Dealership | Dealership | Dealership | VSC |
| Dealership | TPA | Dealership | VSC |
| Dealership | TPA | Insurer | VSC |
| TPA | TPA | Insurer | VSC |
| Manufacturer | Manufacturer | Manufacturer | VSC |
| Insurer | Insurer | Insurer | MBI |

## Obligor Perspectives

It is easiest to begin with manufacturer programs, as the cost to the dealership will likely be the highest. On the surface, one would expect the manufacturer programs to cost the least, since the manufacturer clearly has the best knowledge about its repair costs and expected level of repairs. Therefore, its affiliated insurer would require the least amount of conservatism and risk margin in its pricing.

The paradox is caused by the manufacturers' perspective. While the manufacturer wants to make money on the VSC, its primary orientation is selling more cars—and that means customer satisfaction. The manufacturer program may cost more to the consumer, but once the purchase decision is made, performance is what counts. Manufacturer programs *tend* to provide the broadest coverage in terms of covered repairs and parts. In addition, the manufacturer *generally* has the most liberal claim paying practices. This perspective naturally produces rates that are at the top of the market.

The cost to the dealership of other VSC programs is likely to be less, although the alternative packages can be sold at the same retail cost as the manufacturer program. Can the dealership get the same level of customer satisfaction and pocket greater income? From the marketplace, there is a clear answer—maybe.

Among the dealership choices, the disparity between the lowest available wholesale cost and the manufacturer program is wide. At the low-cost end, the dealership will likely run a high risk of customer dissatisfaction. At some point in the price range, the insurer must restrict coverage or tighten claim-paying practices to maintain profitability. Or even worse, the insurer does neither. Naturally, it's a customer relations problem when part or all of the repair cost is not covered, but at least the insurer is there to answer the phone. Low cost, high benefits and liberal claim-paying practices combined mean disaster to the insurer. The recent demise of regional and national insurers in this marketplace demonstrates that low price is not always the right answer for the dealership.

In general, as the cost to the dealership drops, the ultimate customer satisfaction also drops. However, there are often choices available that reduce the dealership cost while maintaining an acceptable level of customer satisfaction. Finding the optimum choice requires effort. Given a potential *profit* difference of $200.00 or more per contract, the effort is justified.

Assume that the manufacturer program:

- costs the most to the dealership
- is the most comprehensive in coverage
- has the highest sharing of desire for customer satisfaction
- provides a high level of TPA and insurer solvency

If an alternative to the manufacturer program is desired, the goal is to find a TPA/insurer relationship that reduces the dealership cost with an acceptable trade-off in the other criteria. Most TPA/insurer packages provide coverages that are comparable. Have the service department review the contracts and try to understand any differences. Many of the TPA marketing people will have the comparison already done. Be sure to make an independent verification of any comparisons presented to you.

The dealership is the TPA's customer, so "customer" satisfaction generally means consumer satisfaction. While the TPA must say no at times, good administrators can still maintain the goodwill of the consumer.

Clearly the best counsel is the experience of other dealers. Get the references and make the calls. Discuss various programs with other dealers whenever the opportunity arises.

Ask the TPA for references and evidence of financial stability; then ask questions:

- How long has the administrator been in business?
- How knowledgeable are the senior officers?
- Who owns the TPA?
- Does the TPA have a Dun and Bradstreet or other rating?
- Is the TPA regulated by a state agency?
- Does the TPA offer an obligor other than the dealership?

Then consider the insurance protection:

- Who is the insurer?
- What is the Best's rating of the insurer?
- Do the TPA and insurer belong to the same corporate family?

Good marketing people will have the answers to these questions ready for the dealer. Do not be timid about asking for hard copy proof of any oral statements made.

## ANATOMY OF FAILURE

Why do some independent service contract providers fail after four to seven years?

Scores of small service contract providers have failed, but there have been large corporate failures as well, notably UDG, NADS, American Warranty, MIA, Northwest

Underwriters, and General Warranty, to name a few. The

common thread is lack of adequate reserves for *future administrative duties* along with mistaken actuarial loss assumptions. Poor reserving coupled with periodic economic downturns left automobile customers nowhere to turn but to the originating dealership. When the original service contract provider goes broke, this translates into a poor customer satisfaction index (CSI).

The cheapest deal is not necessarily the best deal. Indeed, it is often the worst deal for the dealership and its future CSI. With a natural adversarial relationship between a buyer and seller, the buyer (dealership) wants the most product for the least cost and the seller (service contract company) wants to collect the most for its product. This negotiation process works if the provider of service contracts:

- makes adequate profit **and**
- establishes adequate reserves for future administration and claim losses.

But many dealerships "step over dollars to pick up pennies." They are attracted to a lower cost today without full consideration for tomorrow.

Consider this scenario.

Marketing Driven Service Contract (MDSC) provider starts a business and collects substantial administrative fees in its first year for providing future administrative services. Unfortunately, most of these fees are spent promoting and marketing MDSC itself. After all, other than the cost to convert the initially written service contracts to a computer system format, no claims are presented for the company to adjudicate. In year two, the marketing efforts pay off and the business (new service contracts) increases dramatically, yet there are still few claims from year one's business and virtually none from year two. The company is flying high. Profits are pumped into the marketing machine and year three proves to be better than the other two combined. Claims begin to appear, but it's no real problem. As long as the company continues to increase sales, it pays its claim adjuster employees out of current cash flow. It becomes a self-fulfilling prophecy; spend money on marketing and the business will be a success.

But what is really happening? Are they robbing Peter to pay Paul? The MDSC provider is deluding itself into a feeling of invincibility; it only needs to write more business in order to succeed. More and more money is pumped into marketing efforts on the assumption internal administrative duties will take care of themselves out of current cash flow. Whenever a service contract provider leads its sales materials by boasting about "contracts per month," the dealer needs to be worried. This is an indicator of a marketing-driven corporate philosophy. When the Marketing Driven Service Contract provider's compounded growth rate begins to slow, as it eventually will, either through competitive forces, market saturation, or the periodic economic downturn, profits begin to erode. This occurs just when the wave of claims written from prior years' policies begins to appear, and the claims require adjustment.

In a misguided attempt to salvage the company, MDSC provider turns to its (false) proven record—more efforts and money spent toward sales. It accomplishes this by cutting back internal administration and investing savings into more sales promotion efforts and materials. Slower claim processing results, dealership dissatisfaction increases, and sales do not improve—they deteriorate. The spiral continues downward, perhaps assisted with an economic downturn. The provider fails as a corporate entity.

Rapid growth is the primary warning sign; remember the old school tale about the tortoise and hare? No such thing as a free lunch? Slow, steady growth is a good sign of well-managed service contract providers. In the automobile industry, witness the meteoric growth then virtual collapse of Yugo.

Poor claims turnaround time is a second warning sign for the dealership. This sign may appear too late for the dealership to do anything to protect itself; after all, claims don't begin to manifest themselves in great numbers until service contracts are quite old. If a dealership is experiencing claims adjustment problems for its customers, the dealership most likely has been writing with the same service contract provider for some time. A good man once defined a theorem called the FIRST LAW OF HOLES—*IF YOU ARE IN ONE AND WANT TO GET OUT, QUIT DIGGING!* Make a change for new business as soon as the problems appear.

This looks pretty bleak. On the surface the dealership may conclude that factory programs are the only viable alternative. This may not be the case. Factory programs, while well-funded, are the most expensive alternative for the dealership.

No, there aren't easy answers. Pick the service contract provider carefully. There is a balance between expensive factory-sponsored service contract programs and the cheap "new kid on the block" program. Look at the marketing philosophy of the independent providers of service contracts. Are they adequately capitalized? Do they have a program to reserve adequate funds for future administrative duties? Are they run by honorable people with a good, verifiable track record?

## RETROACTIVE COMPENSATION

Some programs offer the ability to earn additional compensation through a retroactive compensation arrangement. While the feature has some appeal, it does not have the benefits found in a life or disability program. The "payee" under the VSC is the dealership's service department, so a denied claim means money that must be paid directly by the consumer. This may cause consumer dissatisfaction or difficulty in receiving reimbursement.

In addition, the long-term nature of VSCs and conservative insurer reserving practices generally result in a long deferral before any profits show up. Insurers often require pooling of experience among dealers, so the results from other programs impact eventual results. Retroactive compensation is nice when it arrives, but do not make any financial plans that depend on its arrival.

## SELF-INSURANCE

Why not cut out the additional layers of cost and profit and just self-administer and self-insure?

Self-administration has limited appeal. The administrative charge per contract of an administrator/TPA is small. While this charge includes some corporate overhead and profit at the TPA level, it is important to separate the claim adjustment process from the dealership. Even where the dealership is the obligor, the TPA can provide the independence, so that it is the TPA that says "no," rather than the dealership. This position is enhanced when the TPA is the obligor. Any denial will result in some dissatisfaction—the key is to deflect the dissatisfaction from the dealership.

Self-administration does appeal to certain dealers. These dealers believe that if they are doing the administration, they can control the process and ensure customer satisfaction.

In some states, the dealership has the option to self-insure. For long-term financial health, a part of the retail charge must be set aside in a reserve. Then the reserve must be released over time, based on the expected pattern of claims. Maintaining this reserve at appropriate levels requires technical expertise and a tremendous amount of financial discipline when times are tight.

## REINSURANCE

If the dealer owns a domestic property and casualty reinsurer or offshore reinsurer, the primary insurer may offer the option to reinsure the risk into the producer-owned reinsurance company. Both options—self-insurance and reinsurance—have some benefits and substantial risks.

By reinsuring the risks, the reinsurance company owns the reserve fund, even though the fund will be held in custody trust. This means, first of all, that the dealer knows what funds are available. Most insurers are financially stable, but insurers have become insolvent.

With ownership of the funds comes the investment income—a substantial source of income resulting from the payment of premium up front and the three-year to seven-year delay before most claims come due. This flow of investment income is considered when an insurer prices a contract to the dealership, so it is not like "found money." In essence, the dealership receives a portion of this money when the contract is sold. If the insurer did not have investment income, the dealership cost would be much higher.

The pricing risk is real. The vast array of makes, models, mileage limitations, coverages, and manufacturer warranties are a pricing nightmare. Only the manufacturer has sufficient data to be credible for many of the possibilities. Some insurers can make reasonable estimates of the primary pricing options, but the estimates of the alternatives are less precise.

After the premium is collected, it is important to establish an initial reserve that is adequate. The cost of a manufacturer program is a good guide to use in the absence of other reliable information. In a reinsurance program, the primary insurer will require a minimum level and will require that the funds be held in trust.

Once the initial amount is established, it must be earned over the term of the contract. Since VSC protection is similar to automobile physical damage insurance, there is a tendency to earn the premium on a pro rata basis. On a

60-month contract, one-sixtieth of the initial reserve is earned each month, but this is too fast.

**The actual pattern of claims is much different than pro rata**. There are a few claims during the base period warranty and a reduced level during any power train warranty protection. Only when all manufacturer provided protection ceases is the ultimate level approached. Even then, the claim frequency and severity continue to rise. In years three through seven, the claim cost rises, but the rise is moderated somewhat by:

- cars that are sold without a transfer of the VSC
- cars that reach the mileage limitation before the time limitation is reached.

In the absence of actual claim patterns, earning the reserve by the Reverse Rule of 78 (RR78) is the standard answer. The actual pattern, however, is greatly influenced by the manufacturer warranty, so the RR78 is an approximation at best. Most insurers try to measure past experience and to determine the actual pattern of claims. These efforts are only moderately successful. Not only does it take five to seven years to accumulate the data, the dynamic changes that occur in manufacturers' warranties and VSC coverages every few years must be considered.

The bottom line is that VSC pricing and profit evaluation is far from an exact science. It is easy to be fooled, as a number of insurers have demonstrated. The increasing pattern of claims over time can make the profitability appear far more attractive than it is. It really hurts when the claims just keep coming in after the entire premium is gone.

The insurance question is also compounded by federal income tax issues. Under self-insurance, the reserves are not deductible as expenses. The entire retail charge must be included in income in the year sold.

This adverse tax position *may* be overcome in a reinsurance position. Normally, the reserve is deductible at the reinsurance company level, as it would be for any unaffiliated insurance company. The IRS has raised the issue of whether this arrangement constitutes self-insurance. At the IRS level, this situation gets into a much broader issue of reinsurance/self-insurance into true captive reinsurance companies that are owned by a variety of manufacturers for the purpose of reinsuring worker's compensation, group insurance, etc. The IRS position is weak, but that will not stop it from raising the question.

If reinsured, a VSC is a non-life insurance product for tax purposes just like credit disability insurance. Its reserves are non-life reserves and are considered in the test of whether an insurance company is a life insurance company or a non-life insurance company for tax purposes. Its premium income is counted in determining the eligibility for the two small non-life categories. This inclusion may be a positive or a negative feature depending on the optimum tax position, but in any event, it must be considered.

The risks of self-insurance and reinsurance are substantial. These programs are not recommended unless the dealer is committed to maximizing potential for profit with the risk of consumer dissatisfaction and the risk of underwriting losses. Combining the VSC business with credit insurance will expose each product's underwriting hazard to the other's profits.

However, the benefits of self-insurance and reinsurance can be substantial if the dealer understands the liabilities and responsibilities. Get the advice of competent insurance and administrative professionals. Carefully review each proposed program and gain a complete understanding of the benefits and consequences.

# Chapter Thirteen
# Other Aftermarket Sales Opportunities

Automobile dealers have many products to offer after sale of the actual vehicle to enhance back-end profits. These include chemicals, road hazard products, premium equipment enhancements, theft protection devices and other services.

## CHEMICALS

Chemical, or appearance protection, products are defined as those materials that enhance the look and life expectancy of the vehicle appearance. These include fabric protectors, paint sealant, and undercoating to protect against outerbody rust-through. These are typically purchased from independent providers. The product may or may not come with its own unique warranty. In addition to commission on sale of these products, profit margins may be increased by negotiating with the insurance provider of the warranty to reinsure the risk to an insurance company where underwriting profits are available. The chemical business is not quite as popular as it once was because manufacturers are using better metals, paints and fabrics in the manufacturing process, which obviates the consumer need for enhancement products. For example, some manufacturers guarantee their automobile bodies against outerbody rust-through for five to seven years; this duplicates the period of many undercoating companies' coverages. Many of the undercoating providers have dropped out of the business due to this factory competition and the prohibitive risk of the possible carcinogenic nature of the chemicals used.

## ROAD HAZARD PRODUCTS

There are many different innovative products in the road hazard arena, including road clubs (similar to AAA coverage) which feature free towing, rental and bail bond services. There are also some aftermarket providers who supply handy tool kits, tire pumps, flares, etc., which all add to the consumer value received. Dealerships offer these as add-on products to the sale of their vehicles or charge a small fee for these products and services.

## PREMIUM EQUIPMENT ENHANCEMENTS

High-line tires, cellular phone equipment, and fully equipped "jukeboxes" are some of the upgraded equipment offered by the automobile dealership for the consumer's new purchase. This market is also being eroded by manufacturers responding to the obvious consumer demand and filling it with their own products. The dealership is being squeezed out of the premium equipment enhancement marketing opportunity.

## THEFT PROTECTION DEVICES

Given the media barrage about theft of vehicles and equipment, consumers are concerned enough to protect their new investments with anti-theft devices. These anti-theft devices include special keys to disable the ignition, bars that fit over the steering wheel making it impossible to steer the vehicle, and hubcap locks to prevent unauthorized removal. Dealerships either give customers these protective devices as value added to the vehicle purchase or charge a small premium.

## TELE/MAIL PROMPTING

This is a service, provided for dealerships, of periodic calls or letters to vehicle purchasers. It reminds customers of their need for routine warranty maintenance, tire rotation, oil changes, and lubrication. The service sets up a convenient appointment for the customer to bring the vehicle to the dealership where these tasks are performed. The system automatically tracks vehicle usage (average miles per month), then updates itself each time to schedule the next contact based upon actual customer usage projected into the future.

These services are not direct charges to the customer, but rather a technique to generate repeat service work and more sales. The objective is to improve dealership loyalty and service absorption while prospecting for additional sales (e.g., do you know someone who is thinking of trading in a car?).

## INNOVATIONS

In addition to the more traditional products and services listed above, there are some very innovative concepts being offered through today's dealerships. The idea described below is but one of those new products.

Dealerships spend enormous sums of money in print, audio and video advertising to generate showroom traffic. The dealership usually has one shot, then the advertising dollar disappears when that prospect leaves the showroom floor. It's like flying airplanes from point A to B with empty seats—you never recover the lost revenue from empty seats. One innovator is capitalizing on data captured when the customer is on the showroom floor. He developed a successful program to set up appointments and discuss family financial planning. The results are additional revenues of approximately $45.00 to $90.00 per vehicle sold.

The worksheet in Figure 13.1 gives dealerships a quick method to compute how much **MONEY ON THE TABLE** is being left without this type of program. There is no capital expenditure; it costs the dealership nothing. It merely capitalizes upon the enormous amount of data gathered during the automobile sales process.

The dealership of tomorrow needs to maximize its investments. Investments in advertising surely have other collateral product sales opportunities—the successful dealer will open his or her mind to innovative concepts.

## ORDINARY LIFE SALES PRO FORMA

| | |
|---|---|
| (1) Retail Units per Month | ________ |
| (2) Appointment Ratio* | x .10 |
| (3) Potential Appointments | = ________ |
| (4) Sales Ratio** | x .80 |
| (5) Potential Customers Purchasing Insurance | = ________ |
| (6) Average Premium*** | x $800 |
| (7) Total Monthly Premium | = ________ |
| (8) Dealership Commission Rate | x .70 |
| (9) Monthly Income to Dealership | = ________ |

* Appointment Ratio of 10% is one-half of industry norm, based on an agent working a qualified prospect list.

** Eighty percent of all prospects buy an insurance product, based on agents utilizing the Financial Needs Analysis Program with an actual sit-down with customer.

*** Average Premium purchased when presented by the Financial Needs Analysis Program is $800.

---

Note: These pro formas and the figures they contain are for illustration purposes only. No representations or warrants are given, since other uncontrollable variables could affect the figures.



Figure 13.1. Sample life insurance follow-up program.

# Chapter Fourteen
# The Comparison
# Advantages and Disadvantages

## FRONT COMMISSIONS AND RETROS

To evaluate your program, you must consider the front compensation and all of the provisions of any retro arrangement taken together. There is a relationship between the front compensation and various retro programs. It involves a trade-off between guaranteed money and potential additional compensation.

A straight deal is just an up-front commission. This will produce the highest level of guaranteed compensation. The general level of commissions in a state is called the **street commission**. This is the level of commissions paid by most insurers without a retro program.

The way to get the best up-front commission is to talk to other dealers in your state, but remember that your clientele and volume will be different. Listen to the sales pitch from general agents and the direct sales people employed by the insurers. For the most part, there is relatively little difference in the commission rates you can obtain. They will generally fall within a 10% range. Finally, while commissions are important, good service and training take time and cost money. There is real value to doing business with reputable companies who are in the credit insurance business for the long haul. Choose your insurer carefully and do not discard a quality relationship for the hottest deal on the street or the latest reinsurance scheme.

The lesson of Transamerica Life Insurance Company in the 1980s is worth remembering. Before 1985, Transamerica was not active in the automobile segment of credit insurance. It moved into this segment in 1985. For 30 months, it was the hottest company on the street. It paid commissions well above prevailing street commissions. Its production went from virtually nothing to over $200 million on an annualized basis. Transamerica's folly became apparent, and it withdrew from the market entirely after absorbing many millions of dollars of losses. Many credit insurers could not have absorbed this magnitude of losses and would have become insolvent. This is a tough business with narrow profit margins for the insurers. Any company offering significantly more than street commissions is headed for trouble.

Suppose you want more than just the front commission and begin to listen to retro program pitches. You may find insurers willing to offer street commissions and a retro program. This sounds really good, since you have nothing to lose. In fact this is true, but you probably have little to gain. Most of these programs are just window dressing. Upon investigation, you will find most of the programs are based on statutory retros with the least favorable termination provisions. In addition, the administrative fee is set so high that the likelihood of profits is remote. Ask the insurer what it thinks your loss ratio will be. Add your front commission and the administration fee. See how much is likely to be left over.

To create a real upside for you, the insurer will want something in return; a reduction in its risk. Insurers really do not mind sharing the profits, just as long as they are sure there will be profits. The insurer will be satisfied with its fee and the investment income it earns if it feels that the chances of incurring a loss are small. The only way to reduce the risk is to reduce the front compensation. Insurers will want a 10% reduction for a good GAAP retro program. This puts you in a partial reinsurance position. You are forgoing a 10% sure income for a higher potential profit if claims experience is good. Ask your current insurer what your loss ratio is—preferably get a computer printout from the insurer.

If you commit to a retro program, it is to your advantage to work on the quality of your business. Insist that your F&I people are properly trained. If you are not already doing so, begin to track penetration. Ask your insurer or general agent to help. They all have systems in place for you to implement.

Seriously consider underwriting if it is available. Again, get advice from your insurer or general agent. Discuss the problems and advantages with other dealers.

## REINSURANCE

You may want to consider a reinsurance program. This may be your only alternative in commission cap states. Some reinsurance programs are really just a legal form of retros. Make sure you have a clear understanding of the risks involved.

Front commissions and retros involve a simple process at the dealership level—just cash the check. Reinsurance is not so simple. **You must** have at least a general understanding of the risks and rewards—the more understanding the better. Your financial advisor must have a complete understanding.

For many dealerships, reinsurance offers the potential for income that cannot be captured any other way. The investment in time is often well-rewarded. Each deeper level of understanding will open additional profit doors, but the understanding takes time and effort.

## HARD DOLLARS VERSUS SOFT DOLLARS

It is important when comparing various compensation methods to know the kind of money received. In the world of aftermarket sales compensation, there are dollars that *stick* and dollars that are *contingent*. When the dealer makes 100 hard dollars, these can be spent immediately without fear of having a future liability against these dollars. If, on the other hand, the dealer makes 100 soft dollars, some of those dollars are refundable.

A good example of soft dollars is money that is generated as commission from the sale of a cancellable product—credit insurance or service contracts, for instance. In the automobile business, the percentage of refunded credit insurance premiums has been steadily increasing over the years. This is due in large part to the increased term of loans that are offered for higher-cost automobiles. People tire of the vehicle long before the loan expires, and the original coverage is cancelled. This cancellation requires a refund of unearned premiums and dealership commissions.

In the 1990s dealers can expect to refund between 18% and 24% of the credit insurance commissions earned for today's sale, thus the term *soft dollars*. For every $100 in original commission, the dealer can only count on keeping $76 to $82.

An example of hard dollars is investment income. If the dealer can choose between $100 of investment income from reserves on an aftermarket product or $100 from front commission, the choice is obvious. Since $100 of interest is non-contingent, it is worth $100, whereas $100 of commissions is only worth $76 - $82.

## SERVICE CONTRACTS

*Retroactive Compensation.* Retro programs are less prevalent and less rewarding than credit life and disability programs. The likelihood of significant compensation is small and usually comes several years down the road. Such a program has value; just do not depend on the income.

*Self-Insurance and Reinsurance.* These programs are not appropriate for many dealerships. They offer the potential for increased profits, but include the real risks of poor pricing, improper methods of earning the premium over time, and underwriting losses. The downside is significant. If substantial profits are achieved, they may result from restricted coverages and strict claim-paying practices that could result in consumer dissatisfaction in the long run.

Some dealerships have benefited from self-insuring or reinsuring. These are the dealerships that made the investment to fully understand the financial dynamics.

Deal only with experienced general agents and insurer personnel when using one of these mechanisms.

*VSC Provider.* The manufacturer program should be considered and used as the gauge by which to measure the alternatives. *In general,* manufacturer programs provide the lowest compensation to the dealership, but the highest level of benefits and consumer satisfaction. A number of the alternatives will offer the opportunity for increased profits and an acceptable level of consumer satisfaction. However, a number of alternatives are priced such that consumer satisfaction or insurer solvency are at risk. Be wary of the lowest price to the dealership.

In evaluating a TPA/insurer arrangement consider:

- Reputation (talk to friends)
- Experience of personnel
- Years in the business
- Ratings from recognized rating agencies
- Financial strength

# Appendix A
# Glossary of Insurance Terms

NOTE: The definitions in this glossary are the meanings of the words as they apply to credit insurance. Some words also have broader meanings.

**ACCEPTANCE CORPORATION.** A finance corporation formed by an automobile manufacturer to provide financing which is available through the dealership.

**ACCOUNTING DATE.** The "as of" date on which an accounting statement is prepared. The last day of the accounting period.

**ACCRUAL BASIS ACCOUNTING.** The normal basis of accounting for most corporations. The financial statements include the cash transactions, as well as adjustments for income due but not received, expenses incurred but not paid, income received but not earned, and expenses paid but not yet incurred.

**ACTIVE LIFE RESERVES.** A liability of an insurance company representing an estimate of benefits which will be paid after the accounting date on insureds who are in good health on the accounting date, but who will die or become disabled after the accounting date but before the insurance terminates.

**ACTIVELY-AT-WORK CLAUSE.** A policy requirement that the borrower must have worked thirty or more hours per week for one or two months prior to the effective date of the insurance in order to qualify for the insurance coverage.

**ADMINISTRATIVE FEE.** The percentage of gross premiums minus refund premiums retained by the direct writer in a retroactive compensation program for general expenses and profit. It may include premium taxes.

**ADMITTED ASSETS.** Assets which are permitted to be carried on an insurer's statutory annual statement in calculating its net worth. *See also* Basket Clause and Non-Admitted Assets.

**ALIEN INSURANCE COMPANY.** An insurer domiciled in another country.

**ANNUAL PERCENTAGE RATE (APR).** The effective annual rate of interest on a loan.

**ANTI-SELECTION.** The tendency of a borrower, based on his knowledge of his health condition, to select against the insurer when he is deciding whether to purchase insurance coverage.

**ASSUME THE RISK.** To accept the risk on an insurance policy from the direct writer.

**ASSUMING REINSURER.** A reinsurer accepting risk from a direct writer.

**BASKET CLAUSE.** Investments that are accepted as valid assets for statutory accounting that are neither clearly permitted nor prohibited as admitted assets.

**BENCHMARK LOSS RATIO.** In state laws and regulations, the presumed loss ratio on which prima facie rates are based. Also, the loss ratio used to determine whether the benefits provided are reasonable in relation to the premium charged.

**BEST'S RATING.** An insurance company rating given by the A.M. Best Company.

**BILLING METHOD.** A system by which dealerships submit applications at the end of the month to the insurer, who then provides the dealership with a bill for the premiums due minus the dealership's commissions.

**CEDE.** To transfer the risk on an insurance policy from a direct writer to a reinsurer.

**CEDING FEE.** The percentage of gross premiums minus refund premiums retained for general expenses and profit by the direct writer in a reinsurance program. It may include premium taxes.

**CEDING INSURER.** The direct writer who transfers a portion of its risk on an insurance policy to a reinsurer.

**CEDING STATEMENT.** A statement prepared by the direct writer in a reinsurance transaction showing the cash transactions and reserves for the accounting period; *also called* a cession statement or reinsurance cession.

**CERTIFICATE OF AUTHORITY.** Certificate issued by a state or country to an insurer or reinsurer showing that the company is authorized to do insurance business in that state or country.

**CESSIONS.** A ceding statement provided by the direct writer to a reinsurer showing the cash transactions and reserves of the accounting period. The accounting period may be monthly or quarterly.

**CHARGEBACK COMMISSION.** A commission paid by the dealership to the insurer on any premium refunds, equal to the front compensation percentage times the amount of refunds. *Also called* return commissions.

**CLAIM RESERVES.** An estimate of the benefit payments which will be made after the accounting date on claims which have occurred prior to an accounting date. Categories of claim reserves are: incurred but not reported claims, claims in course of settlement, and continuing claims (disability only).

**CLAIMANT.** A borrower covered by a credit insurance policy who files a claim for a loss covered by the policy.

**CLAIMS IN COURSE OF SETTLEMENT (CCS OR ICOS).** Claims which have occurred and have been reported to the insurance company prior to the accounting date, but which have not been paid by that date.

**COINSURANCE.** A reinsurance arrangement by which the risk and all cash elements, except the direct writer's ceding fees, are shared proportionately between the direct writer and the reinsurer. *Also called* quota share coinsurance. *See also* Earned Coinsurance and Written Coinsurance.

**COINSURANCE PERCENTAGE.** The percentage of the original risk that is ceded to the reinsurer.

**COMMISSION CAPS.** State limitations on the maximum compensation paid by insurers to general agents and dealerships.

**1958 COMMISSIONERS EXTENDED TERM (1958 CET).** A mortality table based on a study of 1950-54 experience under an ordinary life insurance non-forfeiture option called extended term insurance. The table is often used to calculate mortality reserves for credit life insurance business.

**CONTINGENT COMMISSIONS.** *See* Retroactive Commissions.

**CONTINUING CLAIMS.** In disability insurance, claims which have occurred prior to the accounting date, and for which the claimants have received at least one disability payment.

**CREDIT DISABILITY INSURANCE.** Disability insurance, purchased in conjunction with a consumer credit transaction, which provides a monthly benefit equal to the required monthly payment, during the continued disability of the insured, during the term of coverage.

**CREDIT LIFE INSURANCE.** Term life insurance purchased in conjunction with a consumer credit transaction, excluding first mortgage loans, which provides a death benefit sufficient to pay off the credit obligation in the event of an insured's death during the term of the coverage.

**DAC TAX.** A requirement that an insurance company establish an asset for tax purposes relating to deferred acquisition costs (DAC). The asset is based on methods prescribed by the IRS rather than actual acquisition costs.

**DEFERRED ACQUISITION COSTS (DAC).** Under GAAP accounting, the portion of expenses paid to acquire the business which may be expensed over the term of the policies. Only those expenses which "vary with and are directly related to" the amount of business produced may be deferred. This includes front commissions and premium taxes. Also called unamortized acquisition expenses.

**DEVIATED RATE.** Any premium rate different from the state's prima facie rate.

**DIRECT WRITER.** The insurance company issuing an insurance policy.

**DISABILITY INSURANCE.** Accident and health protection that provides benefits if the insured is unable to work.

**DISCRIMINATORY DOMICILE RATES.** Premium tax rates levied by some states which are lower for companies domiciled in that state.

**DOMESTIC INSURANCE COMPANY.** A direct writer is a domestic insurer in its state of domicile, i.e., its state of incorporation.

**DOMICILE.** The principal residence of an insurer for legal purposes.

**EARNED COINSURANCE.** A reinsurance arrangement under which the direct writer holds the money and accounts for the transaction on its statutory books as if the business were not reinsured until profits or losses emerge. Earned profits are paid to the reinsurer. If the result is a loss, the reinsurer must reimburse the direct writer.

**EARNED PREMIUM.** The premium dollars collected (or written) for the accounting period, plus the unearned premiums at the beginning of the period, minus the unearned premiums at the end of the period.

**EFFECTIVE DATE.** The day insurance coverage begins, usually the effective date of the loan.

**ELIMINATION PERIOD.** In a disability policy, the specified period a claimant must remain disabled before any benefits are payable. *Also called* the waiting period.

**EVIDENCE OF INSURANCE.** The individual policy or group certificate provided to the insured stating the amount of insurance, premium, term, description of coverage, exceptions, limitations and restrictions.

**EXCESS REINSURANCE.** A reinsurance arrangement where the ceding insurer's loss is limited to a specified dollar amount or to a specified loss ratio. *Also called* stop loss reinsurance.

**EXOTICS.** A reinsurance company with more than one class of common or preferred stock. Each producer of credit insurance owns a class of stock. Profits on each producer's business inure to his class of stock.

**EXPERIENCE REFUNDS.** *See* Retroactive Commissions.

**FINANCE AND INSURANCE SPECIALISTS (F&I PEOPLE).** Individuals employed in automobile dealerships who are trained to handle the financing and insurance matters of an automobile sale.

**FOREIGN INSURANCE COMPANY.** A direct writer is a foreign insurer in every state where it is licensed, except for its state of domicile.

**14-DAY RETROACTIVE COVERAGE.** The most common credit disability coverage sold. The elimination period, or length of time the claimant must remain continually disabled before benefits are paid, is 14 days. Benefits are paid from the first day of disability.

**FRONT COMPENSATION (OR COMMISSIONS).** Guaranteed compensation paid to a general agent or a dealership based on net written premiums for the reporting period.

**GAAP RETROACTIVE COMPENSATION.** Retroactive compensation which is determined by deducting earned commissions.

**GENERALLY ACCEPTED ACCOUNTING PRINCI PLES (GAAP).** The principles of accounting which apply to most U.S. corporations.

**GOOD HEALTH STATEMENT.** A simple form of underwriting wherein the insured signs a statement that says he is in good health to the best of his knowledge and belief.

**GROSS COVERAGE.** Plans of credit insurance which insure the gross indebtedness of a loan.

**GROSS COVERAGE UNIFORM DECREASING TERM INSURANCE.** A credit life benefit that insures the gross indebtedness, paid for with one premium which is charged at the inception of the coverage. The amount of insurance decreases each month by the amount of one monthly payment.

**GROSS LEVEL COVERAGE.** A credit life benefit that insures the gross indebtedness, paid for with one premium which is charged at the inception of the coverage, normally used to insure the residual value of the automobile in a lease transaction.

**GROSS MINUS REFUND PREMIUMS.** *See* Net Written Premiums.

**GROSS UNEARNED PREMIUM RESERVE.** The portion of the original gross premium which represents the remaining premium for the unexpired coverage.

**GROSS WRITTEN PREMIUMS.** Gross premiums collected from the insureds on new insurance issued during the reporting period.

**GROUP POLICY.** In credit insurance, an insurance policy issued to a dealership, where the group is defined as consumers obtaining loans at the dealership. When a borrower is insured, he is enrolled in the group and receives a certificate of insurance as evidence of insurance.

**IN FORCE.** The amount of insurance currently in effect.

**INCEPTION DATE.** The date the dealership first wrote business with a direct writer.

**INCEPTION-TO-DATE.** In a retroactive compensation formula, each element represents the total of all amounts since the dealership began doing business with the direct writer.

**INCURRED BUT NOT REPORTED (IBNR) CLAIMS.** Claims which have occurred prior to the accounting date, but which have not been reported to the insurance company by that date.

**INCURRED CLAIMS.** The total cost of all claims which occur during the accounting period; equal to paid claims, minus the claim reserves at the beginning of the period, plus the claim reserves at the end of the period.

**INCURRED LOSS RATIO.** The ratio of incurred claims to earned premiums, normally expressed as a percentage.

**INCURRED-EARNED LOSS RATIO.** The ratio of the incurred claims to the earned premium, normally expressed as a percentage.

**INDEBTEDNESS.** The amount that is owed.

**INDIVIDUAL INSURANCE.** An insurance contract directly between the insurance company and the person insured, who receives an individual policy as evidence of insurance.

**INITIAL GROSS INDEBTEDNESS.** Initial net indebtedness plus the scheduled interest charges.

**INITIAL NET INDEBTEDNESS.** The total amount advanced, which normally includes the principal of the loan plus the insurance premium.

**INSTALLMENT LOAN.** A loan repayable in substantially equal monthly payments.

**INSTALLMENT SALES CONTRACT.** A debt obligation used to purchase a consumer product which is to be repaid in monthly installment payments.

**INVESTMENT INCOME.** Income generated from the investment of insurance company assets.

**JOINT LIFE INSURANCE.** A credit life insurance policy that insures the borrower and a co-borrower.

**LETTER OF CREDIT.** An obligation issued by a bank which is an unqualified promise by the bank to pay the funds on demand.

**LOSS RATIO.** The ratio of claims to premiums, normally expressed as a percentage. *See also* Paid Loss Ratio, Incurred Loss Ratio, and Incurred-Earned Loss Ratio.

**MONTHLY BENEFIT GROSS DISABILITY COVERAGE.** The usual disability benefit that pays a monthly benefit equal to the monthly loan payment during the continued disability of the insured.

**MONTHLY PAYMENT.** The payment made each month by the debtor to reduce the amount of the loan.

**MORTALITY RESERVE.** Life insurance reserves which are calculated based on a mortality table and an assumed rate of interest. The most common table is the 1958 CET, but other tables include the 1941 CSO Table, 1958 CSO Table, 130% of the 1958 CSO Table, the 1960 CSG, the 1980 CSO Table and the 1980 CET. Used for statutory accounting and tax reserves.

**NET INDEBTEDNESS.** The amount due under a debt obligation at any time. This normally includes the outstanding principal and insurance premium amounts, plus any accrued interest since the last payment.

**NET PAYOFF COVERAGE.** Life insurance protection where the death benefit is equal to the net indebtedness of the loan.

**NET PAYOFF DECREASING TERM INSURANCE.** A credit life benefit that insures the net indebtedness, paid for with one premium which is charged at the inception of the coverage. The benefit is equal to the scheduled outstanding net indebtedness.

**NET WRITTEN PREMIUMS.** Gross premiums collected by the direct writer minus premium refunds paid by the direct writer. *Also called* gross minus refund premiums or G-R premiums.

**NON-ADMITTED ASSETS.** Assets which are not permitted to be carried in an insurer's statutory annual statement in calculating its net worth. *See also* Basket Clause and Admitted Assets.

**NON-RETROACTIVE BENEFITS.** Under a disability policy, benefits which do not include coverage for insured's disability during the elimination period.

**ONE-SIDED REINSURANCE.** *See* Retroactive Commissions.

**OUTSTANDING BALANCE.** The amount of the loan which has not yet been paid the remaining net indebtedness.

**OVERRIDE COMMISSIONS.** Compensation paid to the general agent on the business he produces. It is the difference between the total compensation paid by the insurer and the amount received by the dealership; normally expressed as a percentage of net written premiums.

**PAID LOSS RATIO.** The ratio of paid claims to collected (or net written) premiums, normally expressed as a percentage.

**PENETRATION RATE.** The percentage of eligible borrowers who purchase credit insurance protection.

**PERIOD RETRO.** A method of calculating retroactive compensation where the elements in the calculation show only the amounts during a certain accounting period.

**PREMIUM REFUND.** The unearned portion of the original insurance premium paid to the borrower when insurance on a loan is terminated prior to the scheduled maturity date. *Also called* refunded premiums.

**PREMIUMS.** The consideration paid for the insurance.

**PRIMA FACIE RATES.** Maximum rates adopted by each state which may be used by an insurer without further justification. Each rate is judged "on its face" to produce reasonable benefits in relationship to the premium charged.

**PRINCIPAL (OF A LOAN).** The portion of the automobile's purchase price which is financed.

**PRO RATA.** There are two meanings. The most common meaning is "in equal proportions." The second meaning is "in proportion to."

**PRODUCER-OWNED REINSURANCE (OR INSURANCE) COMPANY.** An insurance company owned or controlled by a dealer for the purpose of insuring or reinsuring the credit insurance business sold by the dealership.

**QUOTA SHARE REINSURANCE.** *See* Coinsurance.

**REFUNDED PREMIUMS.** *See* Premium Refund.

**REINSURANCE.** The transfer of risk from one insurance company, the direct writer, to a second insurance company, the reinsurer.

**REINSURANCE TREATY.** The contract which defines the reinsurance relationship between the direct writer and the reinsurer.

**REINSURER.** An insurance company which accepts the risk on insurance policies written by another insurance company. *See also* Assuming Reinsurer.

**REPORT AND REMITTANCE.** The monthly report provided by dealerships to the insurer showing the business issued and refunds made. Gross premiums are remitted minus refunded premiums and front commissions.

**RESERVES.** An estimate of the future claim payments which will be paid to claimants after an accounting date on business in force on the accounting date.

**RETALIATORY TAXES.** For foreign companies, most states specify that the premium tax rate levied is the higher of:

- the state premium tax rate for foreign companies, or
- the rate charged the state's domestic companies by the foreign company's state of domicile.

**RETENTION.** In standard insurance terminology, the maximum risk an insurer will accept and retain on one life. In credit insurance, it also refers to the ceding fee charged by a direct writer under reinsurance arrangements.

**RETROACTIVE BENEFITS.** Under a disability policy, benefits which are payable from the first day of disability if the claimant remains disabled for the required elimination period.

**RETROACTIVE COMMISSIONS.** Compensation paid to a general agent or dealership which is paid only if his business is profitable and the total commission paid does not exceed the state compensation cap. *Also called* contingent commissions, experience refunds, and retros.

**RETROCEDE.** To transfer risk from one reinsurer to a second reinsurer.

**RETROCESSIONAIRE.** A reinsurer who accepts the risk on insurance policies from another reinsurer.

**RETROS.** Compensation paid to a general agent or dealership which is paid only if his business is profitable and the total commission paid does not exceed the state compensation cap. *Also called* retroactive commissions.

**RETURN COMMISSIONS.** *See* Chargeback Commissions.

**RULE OF 78.** A mathematical formula for calculating the sum of the digits from one to any specified number (n). The formula is:

$$\frac{n \times (n+1)}{2}$$

The sum of the digits from 1 to 12 equals {12 x (13)/2} or 78; *also called* the "sum of digits."

**RULE OF ANTICIPATION.** A method of calculation for refunds where the refund is equal to the premium that would be charged for the remaining term and benefits.

**SCHEDULED INTEREST CHARGES.** The interest charges anticipated over the scheduled loan term calculated at the inception date of the loan.

**SERVICE CONTRACT**. *See* Vehicle Service Contract.

**SINGLE PREMIUM.** One premium charged at the inception of the coverage to pay for insurance.

**STATUTORY ACCOUNTING PRINCIPLES (SAP).** Accounting principles, embodied in state statutes, which are the basis of the statutory financial statements filed annually with the state insurance departments by all U.S. insurers.

**STATUTORY RETROACTIVE COMPENSATION.** A method of determining retroactive compensation whereby paid (written) commissions are deducted.

**STOP LOSS REINSURANCE.** *See* Excess Reinsurance.

**SURPLUS DRAIN.** A temporary loss created under statutory accounting because the premium must be earned over the term of the policy, while expenses are charged when incurred. Even profitable business may result in a loss to net income on the statutory income statement for a period of time.

**TERM OF COVERAGE.** The length of time the insurance will be in force, normally expressed in months.

**TERMINATION DATE.** The last day insurance coverage is in force.

**TOTAL AMOUNT ADVANCED.** The principal plus the insurance premium on a loan.

**UNDERWRITING.** In ordinary insurance, a process of obtaining medical information from insureds and determining whether the proposed insured qualifies as a standard risk or must pay additional surcharges. In credit insurance, the process is far more limited; it could better be described as screening. Risks are either accepted or rejected.

**UNDERWRITING PROFITS.** Premiums less expenses and claims. Expenses include the change in the policy reserves in the accounting period. Claims include the change in claim reserves for the accounting period.

**UNEARNED GROSS PREMIUM.** The portion of the original gross premium representing the value of the unexpired insurance. The portion can be determined using a number of methods, including the Rule of 78s, Pro Rata, or the Rule of Anticipation.

**UNIAGE PREMIUM RATES.** The premium rate is the same for all ages.

**UNISEX PREMIUM RATES.** The premium rate is the same for both sexes.

**UPWARD DEVIATION.** A rate in excess of the state's prima facie rate. To obtain an upward deviation, an insurer must demonstrate that actual experience has produced a loss ratio in excess of the benchmark loss ratio.

**VEHICLE SERVICE CONTRACT (VSC).** An indirect agreement between the customer and the insurer, with the dealership acting as a conduit. The agreement provides protection against premature failure of any covered part.

**WAITING PERIOD.** *See* Elimination Period.

**WALKAWAY COMMISSIONS.** A practice whereby the dealership does not pay back the insurer commissions on refunded premiums. It is more common in Canada than in the United States.

**WALKAWAY VEHICLE SERVICE CONTRACTS.** Service contracts where the insurer retains the risk and does not share the profits with the dealer through retroactive compensation or reinsurance.

**WALKAWAY TERMINATION PROVISION (in a Retro Agreement).** A clause providing that the dealership forfeits all future retros if the relationship with the insurer is terminated.

**WAREHOUSE.** Once a dealer and a direct writer enter into a reinsurance program, the direct writer holds (or warehouses) the business from the effective date of the reinsurance contract until the reinsurance company has been formed.

**WRITTEN COINSURANCE.** A reinsurance arrangement where the risk and the cash elements of the transaction pass from the direct writer directly and immediately to the reinsurer in proportion to the coinsurance percentage.

**WRITTEN PREMIUMS.** Gross premiums collected from the insureds on new insurance less the premium refunds paid to those who terminate their coverage prior to maturity.

# Appendix B
# Glossary of Dealership Terms

**ADD ON.** A method that banks use for computing finance charges on a contract. The amount financed times the add-on interest rate times the number of years equals the finance charge.

**ANNUAL PERCENTAGE RATE (APR).** The true effective interest rate of a loan.

**AS IS.** The automobile has no guarantee whatsoever—it is sold as it stands.

**BABYSITTER.** Term used for a co-signer or co-buyer on an automobile contract.

**BACK END FINANCING.** Contract sent to the bank for financing.

**BALLPARK FIGURE.** A rough estimate.

**B.C.A. (Borrowed Car Agreement).** Form used whenever a dealership lends one of its cars to a customer.

**BEATER.** An old trade-in which is usually "beat up" and worth little or nothing.

**BE BACK.** Prospective buyer who has been in the dealership once or several times and has promised to return.

**BINDER.** A legal form used to bind insurance coverage until a regular policy is issued.

**BIRD DOG.** One who refers prospective customers to a particular dealership or salesman for a given fee or compensation.

**BOOK.** This term refers to the Kelly Blue Book or the N.A.D.A. Book. These books state the wholesale and retail value of any given automobile or truck for the past six years.

**BOUNCE.** To bounce someone means to increase the sales price of the car, the interest rate, or the monthly payments.

**THE BOX.** A room, normally the sales business manager's office, where a deal is finalized before delivery.

**BRICKS.** Refers to a customer's house when it is used as security in taking out a second trust deed loan.

**BROWNIE.** To sell a car to a customer as a result of going around and putting a piece of paper on car windows on the street with a message like "Call me regarding your car."

**BUMP.** *See* Bounce.

**BURIED.** A customer who has too many financial obligations.

**BUY RATE.** The interest rate that banks or financial institutions charge the dealer on contracts being financed.

**CAP.** The maximum interest rate that can be charged on an automobile contract.

**CAP OUT A DEAL.** Complete the transaction–compute the profit, make sure all trade papers are enclosed, fill out DMV forms properly.

**CAPITALIZED COST.** The total cost in a lease agreement before the depreciation or residual value is computed.

**CARRY BACK.** The amount to be financed on any given contract.

**CHARGE BACK.** In the event of an early loan payoff, the bank charges back the dealer's finance reserve, or finance income account, for the amount of unearned income.

**CHERRY.** A vehicle that is clean, immaculate, good-looking, and mechanically sound—just plain good merchandise.

**CHERRY PICK.** When a financing source only approves the excellent or above average customers.

**CHISLER.** Either a regular buyer who constantly grinds the salesman down to the best possible deal, or an individual who floats between dealerships doing nothing but wholesaling cars between dealers.

**CHOKE AND CROAK.** Credit life and disability insurance.

**CHUTE.** *See* Box.

**CLIMBER.** One who is able to tackle tough jobs or tough customers. Used in the phrase, "No hill for a climber."

**CLOSE.** To put the final touches on an automobile purchase to complete a deal.

**CLOSER.** One who closes.

**COLD CANVASS.** A form of prospecting where a salesman or dealership solicits any and all prospective buyers in any given area.

**COMBINATION SALES FORCE.** A sales force that sells both new and used cars, versus having a split force where some sell new cars only and some sell used cars only.

**CONDITION A DEAL.** A deal is normally conditioned when certain requirements must be met, such as an additional down payment, a cosigner or an income verification.

**CO-X.** A cosigner or co-buyer.

**CREAM PUFF.** *See* Cherry.

**CURB.** When a salesman sells his own personal car, or a friend's car, instead of selling one of the dealership's cars.

**TO CURB A CAR.** A salesman who personally buys a customer's trade-in and sells it at a higher price, thus making money for himself and not the dealership. He generally hides it at a distant curb.

**DEALER PREP.** A charge the dealer adds to the price of the car for preparing it for sale after receiving it from the factory.

**DEALER TRADE.** When a dealer will exchange one of his cars with another dealer to meet a customer's likes or requirements in color, equipment, or model.

**DEFERRED PAYMENTS.** Money to be used toward the down payment on a car, which is to be paid after delivery of the car. There is no interest computed on this amount.

**DEHORSE.** When the dealer takes a customer's trade-in and lets him temporarily drive a borrowed car from the dealership until his purchase is completed.

**DESKMAN/DESK.** A man who figures and determines what kind of deal the dealership will make to a customer.

**DETAIL.** Applies to a used car which is cleaned up and made to look as new as possible.

**DEUCE.** Refers to a $200 figure for whatever reason—down payment or trade-in value.

**DIP.** The customer needs part or all of his cash down payment advanced by a finance company.

**DISCOUNT.** The difference between the suggested retail price and the actual purchase price of the automobile.

**DOUBLE DIP.** The customer finances the purchase between two or more loan companies.

**DOWN.** Short for down payment. Also used when a salesman is finished talking to a prospective buyer. He is considered to be down, and the next salesman is considered to be up and in line to handle the next prospective buyer.

**DOWN STROKE.** A customer's down payment.

**DRIVER.** A salesman demonstrator.

**EDGY.** A customer who may or may not be able to get his car financed.

**ETHER.** "Putting someone in the ether" usually refers to a closing situation where the customer is not completely aware of what is happening.

**EYE BALLER.** A flashy-looking, bright-colored, sporty automobile.

**FLAKE.** A customer who usually has bad credit and little or no money for a down payment.

**FLEET.** Usually applies to a multi-car purchase at a substantial discount from the manufacturer's suggested retail price.

**FLIP.** To convert a buyer from financing his automobile through his own bank or credit union to financing through the dealership.

**FLOOR PLAN.** When the dealership's banker or the manufacturer finances the purchase of the automobiles that he has in his inventory.

**FREE & CLEAR.** A trade-in which has no liens on it.

**FRESH POP (DOOR POP).** A customer who has never been in the dealership before and has never been solicited to come to the dealership. He walks in on his own.

**FRONT-LINE READY.** A car that is presentable, both mechanically and in appearance. It is placed in the front line of the dealership's display lot.

**FRONT END.** The customer's down payment, whether he pays it himself or borrows it from a finance company.

**FULL BORE (FULL POP).** To sell a car for sticker price with no discount. If involving a trade-in, not to over-allow on its actual value.

**G.A. (General Agent).** An insurance agent who usually has several appointments with various insurance companies handling various lines of insurance.

**GLAZE.** A finish that is normally put on a new car's paint after it has been cleaned up and made ready for sale.

**GOLD PLATED.** One who has excellent credit and usually has a considerable down payment.

**GRAPE.** A very easy buyer. He is no problem to close and normally goes along with anything anyone tells him.

**GREEN PEA.** A new salesman or sales business manager.

**GRINDER.** A buyer who, no matter what the salesman offers, wants more for less.

**GROSS.** The amount of profit that is realized on a deal prior to deducting sales and delivery expenses.

**GUTS.** Interior of car.

**HANG.** To place a finance deal with one of the various financing sources.

**HARD MONEY.** Actual cash down payment.

**HEN.** Older salesman who adversely influences younger salesman.

**HIGH BALL.** An inflated value given to a prospective customer's trade-in in order to get the customer to return to the dealership to purchase his new car.

**HIGH PENNY.** To adjust a customer's monthly payment, for example, from $223.13 to $223.93. It is safe to assume that if the customer will pay $223.13 for a car payment, he will pay $223.93 without giving it a second thought.

**HOG.** A large, four-door, gas-guzzling, hard-to-sell automobile.

**HOME RUN.** When maximum profit has been made on a deal or when the sales business manager has sold the customer all the aftermarket products he has available.

**HOUSE DEAL.** A purchase that a member of the dealership's management has originated, with no commission to be paid to the salesman.

**HOUSE FINANCING.** A customer's purchase which is financed through the dealership.

**ICE.** Air conditioning.

**INVOICE.** The billing price a dealership pays for a new car from the factory.

**IRON.** An old used car valued at nothing more than the price of iron.

**KINK.** A problem with a deal due to miswriting, misrepresentation, misquoting or mishandling.

**LA-HA.** Credit life and disability coverage which is included in an automobile contract.

**LAID AWAY.** A customer has paid the maximum price for as many items—accessories, financing and insurance—as can possibly be sold on an automobile.

**LAY DOWN.** A customer who says "yes" to everything.

**LINER.** A salesman whose responsibility is to settle a customer on one particular car, get a commitment of some type from the customer, regardless of how ridiculous it is, and then turn the customer over to his T.O. man or sales manager.

**LOAN ROLL.** A used car delivered prior to approval.

**LOSS PAYEE.** The payee under an insurance policy who is first in line for any benefits payable in the event of a loss.

**LOW BALL.** This is a sales figure or tentative price given to a customer who has acknowledged that he is not going to purchase an automobile at this time and wants to shop this figure against other dealerships. This figure is normally unrealistically low, and the automobile cannot actually be purchased for this amount.

**MATURITY.** The length of time for which an automobile is financed.

**MICKEY.** A down payment loan that is arranged by the dealership. This is referred to as "completing a deal in a Mickey Mouse way."

**MINI-DEAL.** A deal with very little profit in it. The dealership normally pays a minimum or flat commission to the salesman for a deal of this type.

**MODIFIED T.O. (MODIFIED TURN OVER).** A sales system which is similar to the straight T.O. system except that the salesman handles the aspects of the sale as long as he is able to close the deal himself. If for any reason he is unable to do this, he then turns the customer over to his sales manager before the customer is allowed to leave.

**MONRONEY.** A new car's window sticker. It was Senator Monroney who introduced the bill in Congress requiring a posted selling price of all new cars.

**MOOCH.** One who knows little or nothing about purchasing, financing or insuring a car and really doesn't care to learn.

**MOTHER.** *See* T.O. Man.

**MOUSE HOUSE.** A finance company.

**MULLET.** *See* Mooch.

**NICKEL.** Refers to $500 for either trade-in value, purchase price or cash down.

**NON-RECOURSE.** A contract written by the dealership where there is no guarantee of the balance by the dealership in any way.

**NOTES.** The monthly payments required for the purchase of any given car.

**ONE-PAY.** A contract where the customer takes delivery of the car and agrees to pay the balance within five to seven days.

**OUTSIDE FINANCING.** When the dealer sends the financing of the automobile through a source where he does not participate in the finance reserve.

**PACK.** Pack is used in figuring a salesman's commission. Depending on the individual dealer, he will deduct anywhere from $75 to $250 from the gross profit of the deal and pay the salesman his commission figured on this difference. Pack also means the salesman or sales business manager quotes to a customer a monthly payment which is inflated to leave room for credit life and disability insurance or other aftermarket products.

**PAPER.** To report the sale of a vehicle and to place the paper report-of-sale on the car. Also, the conditional sales contract on a car. The sales manager is in charge of placing or hanging the paper.

**PAPER DELIVERY.** When all the necessary papers are completed and signed by all parties concerned. The report of sale is placed on the vehicle, and the vehicle is considered sold. However, the customer has not taken physical delivery of the vehicle.

**PAYEE.** One who makes payments on a conditional sales contract whether or not he has signed the contract.

**P.D.I. (PRE-DELIVERY INSPECTION).** Inspection performed by the dealership's service department to ensure that a new vehicle is functioning properly prior to delivery.

**PENCIL.** One definition is when a sales manager pencils a salesman's deal by crossing out the customer's offer and penciling in the figure that he wants to get for that car. The second definition is when a salesman or sales manager changes the selling price or trade-in allowance and covers it up with an increase in the customer's monthly payment because of the additional cost he expects to pay for credit insurance.

**PICK-UP PAYMENT (PICKIES).** The terminology "pick-up" originated in the past when the customer did not have all of his down payment but was able to get the necessary amount, usually within thirty days, at which time he was able to "pick-up" his car. Today, the pick-up payment is now referred to as a *deferred downpayment.* The customer may or may not take delivery of the car prior to this amount being paid.

**PIPE SMOKER.** A customer who smokes a pipe, gives no commitments whatsoever, usually grinds the salesman to his last thread, and doesn't buy the car after all.

**PLAYER.** An individual who is interested in buying a potential customer's trade-in.

**P NOTE.** Personal note, or promise to pay.

**P.O.** Purchase order form used by almost all dealerships to write up the initial sale of a car.

**PRE-COMPUTED.** Method used in figuring the finance charges on a loan or conditional sales contract. To arrive at the customer's monthly payment, the finance charge, computed for the term of the contract, is added to the total note and is then divided by the number of months in the contract.

**PRE-CHECK.** To clear the buyer's credit prior to delivering the car.

**PROSPECT.** A person who is willing and able to buy a car within the next 72 hours.

**PURCHASE DRAFT.** This is similar to a check except that there are normally stipulations printed on the draft which must be met before the bank will pay, such as guarantee of title.

**PUT TOGETHER.** When the sales business manager or sales manager puts together the loose ends of a non-existent deal and makes it a deal.

**R & D (RUST AND DUST).** Chemical treatment to protect paint. Also called Mop and Glow.

**READER.** A check, personal or business.

**RECOURSE.** A contract in which the dealership guarantees repayment to the finance source in the event the customer should default. The terms of this recourse agreement may vary. The most common is called a 90-day repurchase. In the event of delinquency, the finance source has 89 days to get the vehicle back on the dealership's lot and request payment in full of the net balance.

**RESERVE.** The income a dealership realizes on a contract in excess of the finance source's discount rate. For example, if the bank charges $600 in finance charges on a contract and the total finance charge is $1,000, the dealership will realize $400 on reserve.

**RESIDUAL.** The termination value of a leased automobile.

**RETAIL.** The way the average individual purchases an automobile.

**ROLL.** To deliver a car to the customer.

**ROLL BACK.** To work a deal backwards. Instead of working with the purchase price and trying to determine a monthly payment, the salesman starts with a known monthly payment and tries to determine a selling price.

**R.S. (REPORT OF SALE).** Licensing the vehicle in the new owner's name.

**RUBBER.** Tires.

**RULE OF 78s.** A mathematical formula used in figuring a refund of unearned charges of prepaid premium.

**SHOPPER.** An individual who has admitted he will not buy a car until he has shopped other dealerships to be sure he is getting the best possible price.

**SHORT RATE.** The computation of rebates on insurance policies prior to their expiration. The mathematical formula is the same as the Rule of 78s.

**SIX-PACK.** Combination packet containing all necessary papers needed for a customer to sign in order to transfer ownership of his trade-in. This packet includes The Notice of Sale or Transfer of Interest and Federal Odometer Disclosure combined into one, the Bill of Sale, Authorization for Payoff, Payoff Adjustment, and Power of Attorney.

**SKATE.** What one salesman does to another. For example, a customer comes to the dealership and goes through the motions of checking out a car without deciding whether or not to buy. He returns and asks for the same salesman. The salesman who greets the customer the second time tells him the salesman he wants is not there, but he (the second salesman) can help him complete the purchase of the car. The second salesman then forgets to tell the sales manager of the first salesman's involvement in the deal. Therefore, instead of splitting the commission on the deal, the second salesman takes it all.

**SLED.** An old trade-in which is usually "beat up" and worth little or nothing.

**SLIDE RULER.** A buyer who is a specification nut. He does not deal in generalizations when prices are quoted. They must be exact and justified most of the time. This buyer will have a pocket calculator with him to calculate his own sales tax and total sales price.

**SOFT.** Reference to a used car regarding its salability. There is little or no market for the car and, if sold, the price is generally below the wholesale Blue Book value.

**SPEAR.** A method used to get a customer onto a dealer's lot. For example, stopping a man on the street and telling him that you would give him some outrageous figure for his trade-in, if he would just come down to the dealership today and take a look at what you have to offer.

**A SPLIT.** Sales commissions arising from one sale divided between two salesmen.

**SPOT DELIVERY.** When all phases of the purchase and delivery are completed the same day. This may be with or without any kind of credit check.

**STICKS.** The borrower's furniture which is used as collateral on a small loan.

**STRAIGHT-SELL.** This method of selling is the oldest. The salesman, and usually *only* the salesman, handles the complete transaction from selling the car to delivering it.

**STRAW PURCHASE.** When a third party buys an automobile and finances it in his name because of the actual driver's age, bad credit or lack of credit.

**STROKER.** An individual who gives the impression that he wants to buy a car but really doesn't have the means to do so.

**STROKES.** The monthly payments on the conditional sales contract for the purchase of a car. For example, "The strokes on that Camaro are $195 a month."

**STRONG.** When used in reference to an automobile, it indicates that the car is a good seller, and an above average profit can normally be made on it. The second application refers to a sales individual, reflecting his ability to do his job.

**STUD.** *See* second application of "Strong."

**SWITCH.** To persuade a customer to buy a different car from what he was originally considering because of availability or possible profit.

**TAGS.** The license plates required on the automobile.

**THIRD BASEMAN.** An individual who accompanies a prospective buyer because the buyer feels that person is better versed in haggling over the price of the car or knows more about the car mechanically, thereby decreasing the chances of getting stuck with a lemon.

**TIRE KICKER.** An individual who doesn't want to buy a car but wants to look. He walks in, touches the merchandise, and doesn't want to talk to anyone.

**T. AND L.** The tax and license required in the purchase of a given automobile.

**TISSUE.** The retail price posted on the window of a new car.

**T.O. (TURNOVER).** The procedure used in selling where the salesman or liner turns a prospective buyer over to another salesman or sales manager to close the sale.

**T.O. MAN.** The individual to whom a salesman or liner will turn a customer over.

**TOAD.** A trade-in which is a worn-out piece of machinery—just "sitting there" like a toad.

**TOTE THE NOTE.** A deal where the dealership provides the financing. Particularly common on "Buy here, Pay here" lots.

**TRIP.** To deliver the automobile to the prospective buyer; to "trip a car."

**U.G.** To unconditionally guarantee re-purchase of a conditional sales contract whenever that contract should become overdue.

**UNDER-ALLOWANCE.** To give a customer less for his car than it is actually worth.

**UNWIND.** To take back a car that is already delivered and void all papers that were used in reference to its delivery.

**UP SYSTEM.** System used in greeting prospective customers. The salesmen's names are listed and as the top man on the list greets a prospective buyer, his name is crossed off and the next salesman becomes the "up man."

**UP-RATE.** To increase an individual's rate on his automobile insurance, either due to an error when initially rating the customer or a difference in the customer's driving record from what was originally stated.

**UPSIDE-DOWN.** When a customer wants more on his trade-in than the car is worth.

**WALKING FIGURES.** When the salesman knows for sure that the customer will not buy a car at this time because he wants to check out some other dealerships. The salesman gives him a ridiculously low figure to try and beat the other dealerships, knowing that in the end the customer will have to come back to him.

**WATER.** The false equity shown on a deal that a customer is supposed to have in his trade-in.

**WHEELS.** An automobile.

**WINDOW.** The retail price posted on the window of a new car as required by the Federal Government. The vehicle cannot be sold for more than this price.

**WHOLESALE.** First, the method used in selling a customer's trade-in. Second, to purchase used cars through an individual or at an auction.

**WOULD YA, COULD YA.** A practice used by salesmen in getting a commitment from a customer. In other words, "Would you buy this car if I could get it for the price you want to pay?"

# Appendix C
# Sample Reinsurance Treaty

The following document is a sample reinsurance treaty of the Direct Writer Life and Casualty Insurance Company with a producer-owned reinsurance company. Each Article in the treaty is reviewed in detail, with the commentary shown in italics.

---

**WAREHOUSING and REINSURANCE TREATY**

TREATY NUMBER____ EFFECTIVE DATE __/__/__

THIS AGREEMENT is made by and between Direct Writer Life and Casualty Insurance Company, Anytown, USA (hereinafter called "DWL"), and

______________________________

NAME

______________________________

ADDRESS

______________________________

CITY, STATE, ZIP

a producer of credit life and credit disability insurance coverages (hereinafter called "Producer"), and

NAME

UNITED STATES ADDRESS

CITY, STATE, ZIP

an insurance company (hereinafter called "InsCo"), to be appointed by Producer, which will reinsure certain risks of DWL under the terms and conditions contained within the Reinsurance portion of this Agreement.

*This basic entrance to the treaty identifies the Treaty Number and the Effective Date of the treaty. Next, the parties to the Agreement are identified and given pseudonyms. These pseudonyms are used throughout the remainder of the document.*

*TREATY NUMBER. This is a unique identifier assigned by DWL to this treaty.*

*EFFECTIVE DATE. The Effective Date of the Agreement controls the date of the first policy or certificate to be warehoused and ceded under the treaty. If the Effective Date is 11/1/92, the first policy with an effective date of coverage that is the same as or later than this date is covered by the treaty. POLICY AND CERTIFICATE EFFECTIVE DATES CONTROL WHETHER THE RISK IS CEDED OR NOT. To illustrate, assume a batch of policies or certificates is received by DWL on December 1, 1992. In that batch, the effective dates of the risks are from October 1 through November 15.*

*Only those policies/certificates with effective dates of November 1 and later will be covered by this treaty. All others will be retained by DWL.*

*A dealer already writing business with DWL may want to negotiate this date; however, DWL will rarely "back date" the arrangement before the current year. As part of the negotiation to salvage an existing account, DWL may agree to back date the warehousing function to a time before the actual negotiation. This is an especially powerful negotiating tool available to DWL. For example, if a large producer is being courted by an aggressive competitor with a reinsurance program, DWL may be able to retain the account by offering something that no competitor can offer—cession of premiums already booked by DWL. The dealer must think hard about leaving something of value by changing carriers. The effective date of the treaty will be the agreed-upon date for the risk cessions. The computer system will automatically look back and cede those previously booked premiums and claims to the reinsurer.*

*CONTRACTING PARTIES. The first party to this Agreement is Direct Writer Life and Casualty Insurance Company, the U.S. domestic insurer whose name is on the actual insurance certificates. Sometimes these cessions are made through an intermediary company. For example, DWL may cede all of its reinsured business to a single offshore insurer that retrocedes it to the individual producer-owned reinsurers.*

*The second party to this contract is a person or entity that controls the placement of credit insurance business. This may be an automobile dealer or a general agent. This second party to the contract assumes the pseudonym of "Producer."*

*The third party to the contract is not named immediately unless the Producer has already formed (or selected) a reinsurance company to assume the risks ceded by DWL. Typically, the Producer will form this insurance company. Often, at the time of the contract signing, the name has either not yet been chosen or it has not been approved by the regulatory authorities in the domicile of the reinsurer. The pseudonym used throughout the remainder of the treaty for the reinsurance company is "InsCo."*

WITNESSETH

The parties hereto acknowledge that this is a two-phased Agreement, the first being the Warehousing portion and the second being the Reinsurance portion. Further, Producer and DWL agree that InsCo will be named within a reasonable time by Producer and that this appointment, plus acceptance of the terms and conditions of the Reinsurance portion of this Agreement by InsCo, shall signal an automatic end to the Warehousing phase and the beginning of the Reinsurance phase of this Agreement. It is further understood and agreed that either Producer or DWL may elect to forgo entry into the Reinsurance portion by exercising their respective termination rights within the Warehousing portion of this Agreement.

*The opening paragraph of this contract makes it clear that the treaty is two separate but integrated agreements—a warehousing portion and a reinsurance portion. Operation of these two phases is mutually exclusive; the reinsurance provisions will never be activated under this treaty until the warehousing phase has been terminated.*

*An event is defined that signals the end to the warehousing phase and entry into the reinsurance phase. This identifiable event is acceptance of the terms and conditions of the reinsurance portion of the treaty by an officer of the reinsurance company (InsCo) designated by the Producer. Prior to that time, however, either of the other two parties to the treaty may exercise its right to terminate the warehousing phase, thus electing to forgo entry into the reinsurance phase.*

WAREHOUSING PORTION - ARTICLE I

DWL hereby agrees that it shall issue or assume certain credit life and credit disability insurance risks on and after the effective date of this Agreement offered through the producers specifically identified under the Account Numbers listed on the attached Schedule of Account Numbers. DWL further agrees to hold these risks until such time as the Reinsurance portion of this Agreement is entered, at which time DWL agrees to cede these risks to InsCo under the terms and conditions of the Reinsurance portion of this Agreement.

*This Article spells out that DWL will immediately accept insurance risks from certain dealerships named in the attached Schedule of Account Numbers. These risks are further defined in the Schedule of Account Numbers by identifying the "account numbers" assigned by DWL and the effective dates of the risks to be ceded. Typically, this effective date will be a duplication of the treaty effective date. However, some situations can occur that will call for other effective dates. In that instance, the date on the Schedule will supersede the treaty effective date ONLY FOR THAT PARTICULAR ACCOUNT.*

*DWL further agrees to hold the risks assumed until such time as the Producer has appointed a reinsurance company to assume the risks, as evidenced by an officer of the appointed reinsurance company (InsCo) executing this treaty. At that time, DWL will cede the risks to InsCo under the terms and conditions stated in the reinsurance portion of the treaty.*

WAREHOUSING PORTION - ARTICLE II

As consideration for DWL to hold the credit life and credit disability insurance risks until an insurance company is selected and appointed by Producer, Producer agrees that it shall use its best efforts to assure that the sub-producers identified in the attached Schedule of Account Numbers offer only the credit insurance policies issued by DWL.

*As consideration for DWL to assume and hold the risks under this treaty, the Producer agrees to make a genuine effort to convert the accounts listed in the Schedule of Account Numbers to DWL. This feature recognizes logistical problems involved in conversion of credit insurance accounts to a new insurance company. It is mainly designed so that a Producer can have a reasonable period of time to convert these accounts to DWL paper. However, it does place the contractual burden on the Producer to offer DWL products exclusively.*

*This feature will give DWL a degree of assurance that the Producer intends to form a reinsurer willing to accept the insurance risk. It will give an out to DWL if the Producer is selecting against DWL by submitting only higher risk business to DWL under this Agreement. In order for the Producer to do this, there must be more than one carrier per account, thus violating the "exclusive use" provisions of this Article.*

## WAREHOUSING PORTION - ARTICLE III

This Warehousing portion of the Agreement shall remain in effect until automatically terminated by entry into the Reinsurance phase. Entry into the Reinsurance phase shall automatically occur when a reinsurance company has been appointed by Producer and that company accepts the terms of the Reinsurance portion by executing this Agreement.

However, this Agreement may be terminated sooner by either DWL or Producer by written notification as defined herein. If terminated by written notification, the entire Agreement shall terminate and there shall be no further obligations of either Producer or DWL to the other.

Either Producer or DWL may terminate this Warehousing phase, thus preventing entry into the Reinsurance portion, by giving one hundred twenty (120) days prior written notification to the other at their respective addresses listed within this Agreement. However, it is understood and expressly agreed that should the written termination provision be exercised by either party, and Producer selects and appoints a reinsurance company and causes that company (InsCo) to execute this instrument before expiry of the notification period, this written termination of the Warehousing portion shall automatically become null and void, since at that point the Warehousing activity terminates and the Reinsurance phase automatically beings.

*This final Article of the warehousing portion of the Treaty defines how long the activity will continue. It also defines that the activity will be terminated in one of two ways–either by appointment of a reinsurance company (InsCo) and acceptance of the reinsurance portion of the Agreement by InsCo, or by either party electing to terminate the Agreement.*

*However, there is a problem with a concept of termination that is resolved in this Article. For example, DWL can be unjustly enriched by terminating this Agreement, thus preventing entry into the reinsurance phase and causing the underwriting profits that rightly belong to the Producer (through the reinsurer InsCo) to revert to DWL. To assure that this does not happen, the Producer only needs to appoint InsCo and have InsCo execute the Agreement before the end of the 120-day period. If that occurs, the execution of the Agreement by InsCo overrides the written notice of termination rendered by DWL.*

*There will be few instances when DWL will want to terminate a relationship in this manner. One principal reason is if the Producer is submitting poor quality business. By sending notice of termination, DWL forces the Producer to "put up." If the Producer believes that the block of business has inherent deferred profit, a reinsurance company can be designated to assume the risks already booked. If that occurs, DWL should not care so long as the designated reinsurer, InsCo, faithfully performs its obligations under the reinsurance portion of the Agreement. Even if the Producer overrides DWL's attempt at termination during the warehousing portion of the Agreement, DWL still has an option to terminate this treaty in the reinsurance portion of the contract.*

REINSURANCE PORTION - ARTICLE I

As inducement for DWL to enter this Reinsurance portion of the Agreement with InsCo, Producer agrees to continue to use DWL for all credit life and credit disability insurance risks of the sub-producers identified in the Schedule of Account Numbers for a minimum period of thirty-six (36) consecutive months from the date of the first Ceding Statement.

DWL hereby cedes and InsCo hereby accepts as reinsurance 80% of DWL's liability on any one life under all credit life and credit disability insurance issued or assumed by DWL on and after the effective date of this Agreement and identified under the Schedule of Account Numbers. The life insurance liability ceded hereunder shall be called "said life insurances"; the disability insurance ceded hereunder shall be called "said disability insurances"; and the life and disability ceded hereunder shall be collectively called "said insurances."

*This Article is designed to prevent the Producer from using DWL as a temporary testing ground to determine the profitability on a block of business, obtaining that profit, and then walking away. In other words, this Article precludes a dealer from warehousing business for a few months or years, building up a nest egg of underwriting profit and obtaining that profit by entering the reinsurance phase with no intention of establishing a continuing relationship with DWL. This Article says to the dealer / agent, "If you want all the profits inherent within the warehoused business, you must continue to exclusively write through DWL for a minimum period of thirty-six months AFTER THE FIRST CEDING STATEMENT IS RENDERED." If this obligation is not adhered to, the Producer and InsCo have forfeited their rights to any future underwriting profits that may be earned on the block of business.*

*The second section defines the quota share arrangement for the risk to be ceded to InsCo. In this example, eighty percent of the life and disability risk is to be ceded from DWL to InsCo under the terms of this treaty. This can be easily modified to provide any quota share percentage desired.*

REINSURANCE PORTION - ARTICLE II

As reinsurance premium for said life insurances, DWL shall pay InsCo an amount equal to the gross premiums received for said life insurances less return premiums thereon. InsCo shall allow DWL a ceding commission equal to the sum of

- 15% of the excess of the gross premiums over the return premiums on said life insurances, plus
- the sum of all commissions paid or allowed by DWL on said life insurances, plus
- the sum of all taxes paid by DWL on said life insurances.

If return premiums exceed gross premiums written, InsCo will return to DWL the excess minus the ceding commission and taxes previously retained by DWL.

As reinsurance premium for said disability insurances, DWL shall pay InsCo an amount equal to a percentage (specified in the attached Schedule of Percents as "Percent Written") of the gross premiums received for said disability insurances less return premiums thereon, plus a percentage (specified in the attached Schedule of Percents as "Percent Earned") of the premiums earned by the pro rata method for said disability insurances. InsCo shall allow DWL a ceding commission equal to the sum of

- 15% of the reinsurance premiums on said disability insurances, plus
- the sum of all commissions paid or allowed by DWL on the reinsurance premium, plus
- the sum of all taxes paid by DWL on the reinsurance premium for said disability insurances.

*This Article defines the amount of premium paid to InsCo for its assumption of the risk. The life premium allowed is equal to all of those premiums collected on "said life insurances." "Said life insurances" has been previously defined as the amount of life insurance ceded; in this treaty that equals 80% of Direct Writer's risk. This means that the premium paid to InsCo is 80% of that collected by DWL. This premium is computed on a written premium or paid basis.*

*The premium allowed for disability is likewise a function of "said disability insurance"; in other words, 80%. The difference between the life and disability reinsurance premiums is that a portion of the disability premiums is ceded on an earned premium basis rather than on a written premium basis. As InsCo's financial situation permits, DWL can adjust the portion of the disability premiums ceded on a written basis. As the percentage of the disability premiums ceded on a written basis changes, the Schedule of Percents attached to the treaty will be updated.*

*As a deduction from the reinsurance premium, DWL will take a ceding commission equal to:*

1. *15% of the reinsurance premium, plus*

2. *the sum of all commissions paid or allowed, plus*

3. *the sum of all taxes (this includes premium tax and any other applicable taxes).*

*For life and disability, this ceding commission is a percentage of the reinsurance premium.*

REINSURANCE PORTION - ARTICLE III

On or before forty-five (45) days after the close of the calendar quarter in which InsCo executes this Agreement with respect to the period from the first policy effective date hereof through the end of that calendar quarter, and on or before forty-five (45) days after the end of each calendar quarter thereafter with respect to business received during that quarter until all liability under this Treaty has expired and all losses have been paid, DWL shall submit a Ceding Statement to InsCo giving the following information with respect to the said insurances:

1. Reinsurance premium

2. Ceding commissions

3. Losses and allocated loss expenses. Allocated loss expenses shall be defined as those expenses incurred in excess of the normal expense of supervision, investigation and defense of claims arising under this Reinsurance Treaty.

4. Claim reserves at the end of the accounting period less claim reserves at the beginning of

the accounting period (reserves include those for incurred but unreported losses).

5. Cancellation reserves at the end of the accounting period less cancellation reserves at the beginning of the accounting period.

6. Premiums due and unpaid from Account Numbers listed on the attached Schedule of Account Numbers, less ceding commissions due thereon.

7. Insurance data (number of policies and amount of insurance):

   a. issued during the period

   b. refunded during the period

   c. expired

   d. terminated by death

   e. in force at the end of the period

8. Policy reserves on said life insurances inforce at the end of the accounting period and a percentage (specified in the attached schedule as "percent written") of the pro rata unearned premium policy reserves on said disability insurances.

If Item 1 exceeds the sum of Items 2, 3, 4, 5 and 6, DWL shall remit such excess to InsCo upon submission of such Ceding Statement. If Item 1 is less than the sum of Items 2, 3, 4, 5 and 6, InsCo shall pay such difference to DWL within five (5) days after receipt of the Ceding Statement.

InsCo shall maintain on deposit the amount of Item 8 in accordance with the terms of the Safekeeping Agreement attached hereto as Exhibit A. In any quarter in which an additional amount must be deposited to bring the total amount on deposit to the required sum, DWL may place on deposit such additional amount and such deposit will constitute payment, to the extent of the deposit, of any amount due from DWL to InsCo hereunder. However, DWL may, in its own discretion, demand that InsCo bring the amount on deposit to the required sum within five (5) days after receipt of the Ceding Statement.

*This Article fully defines the ceding statement and quarterly financial responsibilities of each party. The date of the first ceding statement is defined as being on or before forty-five days after the end of the quarter in which InsCo becomes a bona fide insurance company. A Certificate of Authority to transact business, issued by the appropriate regulatory authority having jurisdiction over InsCo, must be submitted to DWL by InsCo before the first ceding statement is prepared. Subsequent statements should be made in a regular manner within forty-five days after the end of each calendar quarter. This forty-five-day period is needed to assure that adequate time is available for all of the administrative and accounting activities necessary to render an accurate statement.*

*DWL will be responsible for submitting quarterly statements to InsCo until after the last policy has expired and the last claim has been paid. The information on the statements will consist of the eight items listed in this Article.*

*The flow of funds between these two parties will be governed by the mathematics described in this Article. Also, the timing of the flow of funds between the two entities is defined in this Article.*

*This Article also defines the responsibility of InsCo to post life mortality reserves and a portion (if any) of disability unearned premium reserves in a Safekeeping account, described in detail in a Safekeeping Agreement attached to the treaty. This account will be structured in such a manner that InsCo will enjoy all of the investment income earned on the policy reserves reinsured. DWL will withhold from each cession the amounts necessary to post loss reserves and cancellation reserves, and will be entitled to the investment earnings on these funds. Cancellation reserves are amounts withheld from the cession to reflect the fact that the amount to be refunded for credit life insurance terminated by early payoff of indebtedness is often greater than the mortality reserve. These amounts are prudent for DWL to withhold from the cession to a reinsurance company with a limited amount of capital and surplus.*

*Notice that one of the deductible items (number six) gives DWL the right to deduct any premiums due and unpaid by any Producer from the reinsurance premiums due to InsCo for any cession. This gives DWL another automatic right to cure a default by a dealership.*

REINSURANCE PORTION - ARTICLE IV

DWL shall furnish such details in connection with said quarterly statements as may be requested by InsCo in order to comply with the requirements of any regulatory authority having jurisdiction over InsCo. InsCo shall at all times have full and free access during business hours at the United

States administrative office of DWL to all books, records and files relating to business covered by this Treaty.

*This Article contains typical treaty terminology that allows reasonable access by InsCo to all information related to the business covered by the treaty. This access is intended to allow regulators and auditors of the reinsurer (InsCo) to examine any of the details of business ceded to date—claims paid, policies booked, etc. The Article guarantees access to that information at reasonable times.*

REINSURANCE PORTION - ARTICLE V

DWL furnishes InsCo herewith specimen forms upon which all said insurances shall be written and will promptly notify InsCo of all changes in said forms. The supervision and payment of all claims under said insurance shall be handled by DWL or its assignee. The liability of InsCo shall follow the liability of DWL in accordance with the terms and conditions of said insurances.

*So that there are no misunderstandings about the underlying contracts of insurance covered by this reinsurance Agreement, InsCo acknowledges receipt of copies of the relevant policy forms. Also, this Article provides that DWL will promptly give InsCo a copy of any replacement or additional policy forms that will come under the terms of this treaty. If there is a change in the insurance risk brought about by the new policy forms, InsCo can, presumably, have the option not to reinsure those risks. This Article also specifically defines that the liability of DWL is the liability of InsCo.*

## REINSURANCE PORTION - ARTICLE VI

In the event of insolvency of DWL, the insurance under this Treaty shall be payable, without diminution because of DWL's insolvency, by InsCo to DWL's liquidator, receiver or statutory successor on the basis of the claim or claims allowed on said insurances against the insolvent DWL by any court of competent jurisdiction or any justice or judge thereof, or by any liquidator, receiver or statutory successor having authority to determine and allow such claims. It is agreed, however, that the liquidator, receiver or statutory successor of DWL shall have to give written notice to InsCo of the pendency of a claim against DWL on this Treaty within a reasonable time after such claim is filed in the insolvency proceeding and that during the pendency of such claim, InsCo may investigate such claim and interpose, at its own expense, in the proceeding where such claim is to be adjudicated any defense or defenses which it may deem available to DWL or its liquidator, receiver or statutory successor. The expense thus incurred by InsCo shall be chargeable, subject to court approval, against DWL as part of the expense of liquidation to the extent of a proportionate share of the benefits which may accrue to DWL solely as a result of the defense undertaken by InsCo.

*The purpose of Article VI is to describe the details of a transaction that will occur if DWL becomes insolvent. This Article specifies the obligation of DWL's liquidator, receiver or statutory successor to promptly notify InsCo in the event of a claim. It also defines the rights and liabilities of InsCo in such an event.*

*Even if DWL is found to be insolvent, the obligations of InsCo must continue to be met in full, as if DWL were a solvent and viable entity. If InsCo steps into the shoes of DWL to adjudicate claims, its expense (as it relates to the portion of the risk retained by DWL) takes priority in the bankruptcy proceedings for payment.*

REINSURANCE PORTION - ARTICLE VII

In the event of insolvency, bankruptcy, receivership, rehabilitation or liquidation of InsCo, DWL may retain all or any portion of any amount then due or which may become due to InsCo under this Treaty, and such amounts, in addition to amounts held and/or due under the Safekeeping Agreement, may be used for the purpose of paying any and all liability hereunder until it has been discharged, at which time DWL shall pay to InsCo, its liquidator, receiver or statutory successor the balance of such amounts withheld as may remain, provided that no default by InsCo has occurred, in which case InsCo, its liquidator, receiver or statutory successor shall forfeit any amounts which remain.

*Article VII identifies the rights and obligations of DWL in the event that InsCo becomes insolvent. Essentially, DWL may, at its discretion, seize the policy reserves under the Safekeeping Agreement and discharge the obligations of InsCo. All funds remaining after discharging these responsibilities will then be turned over to the liquidator, receiver or statutory successor of InsCo, provided there has been no default by InsCo under the Agreement. This would mean that while InsCo is in rehabilitation, it must fully pay all monies due to DWL and otherwise fully comply with the Reinsurance Treaty or risk leaving all underwriting profit "on the table." Thus, InsCo cannot merely shut is doors and wait until all policies expire. If InsCo is in the risk business, it must accept the potential liability of loss, even though it is in rehabilitation, in order to enjoy any possible gain.*

## REINSURANCE PORTION - ARTICLE VIII

All disputes and differences between the two contracting parties upon which an amicable understanding cannot be reached are to be decided by arbitration. The arbitrators shall regard this Agreement from the standpoint of practical business and equity rather than from that of strict law.

The court of arbitrators, which is to be held in the city of Anycity, Anystate, shall consist of three (3) arbitrators who must be current or former executive officers of insurance companies other than the two parties to this Agreement. One of the arbitrators is to be appointed by DWL, the second by InsCo, and the third is to be selected by those two representatives before the beginning of the arbitration. Should one of the parties decline to appoint an arbitrator or should the two arbitrators be unable to agree upon the choice of the third, the appointment shall be left to the Executive Vice President of the Consumer Credit Insurance Association.

The arbitrators are not bound by any rules of law. They shall decide by a majority of votes, and from their written decision there can be no appeal. The cost of arbitration, including the fees of the arbitrators, shall be borne by the losing party unless the arbitrators shall decide otherwise.

*This Article states that any disputes arising under the terms of the Agreement are resolved through arbitration. There is no valid reason to subject complicated and often misunderstood subjects, such as credit insurance and reinsurance, to adjudication by the court system and lay people. This avoids the arduous and expensive process of educating a judge and jury to the nuances of insurance mechanics. This Article provides that three officers of insurance companies, preferably those familiar with credit reinsurance, be selected to resolve any disputes.*

*Each of the parties, DWL and InsCo, must choose one arbitrator and those two will choose a third. Should the two arbitrators be unable to agree on selection of the third, the Executive Vice President of a respected and unaffiliated insurance organization will select the third arbitrator.*

*This Article directs the decision-making process. Arbitrators should not interpret this Agreement in its literal context, but rather from a point of equity. They must direct their efforts to determining what the parties intended when they executed this treaty.*

REINSURANCE PORTION - ARTICLE IX

This Treaty constitutes the entire contract between the parties related to the subject matter hereof and may, by mutual consent, be altered in any of its terms and conditions by a signed addendum hereto.

This Treaty may be terminated without cause by DWL upon ninety (90) days written notice to InsCo. InsCo may terminate this Treaty without cause upon ninety (90) days written notice to DWL after the first thirty-six (36) month period immediately following the first ceding statement rendered by DWL to InsCo hereunder.

Upon termination without cause, the terms of this Treaty shall apply to all said insurances issued before the date such termination becomes effective until their expiry or cancellation in the normal course of business.

This Treaty may be immediately terminated by DWL in the event of default by either Producer or InsCo of any of the covenants contained within this Reinsurance portion. In the event of such termination, Producer and InsCo forfeit all rights to future profit which may inure hereunder and DWL may, at its sole option, recover all of the amounts deposited in accordance with the terms of the Safekeeping Agreement.

*Article IX specifies that this contract is the entire contract between the parties on the subject matter. There are no additional contractual agreements that pertain to the reinsurance transactions under this Agreement. Any changes in the contract must be in the form of a written addendum, agreed to and signed by all parties. The termination provisions are also specified in this Article. Either DWL or InsCo can terminate this Agreement with ninety days prior written notice. InsCo does have the additional constraint that it cannot exercise its termination provision until after the minimum thirty-six-month period has elapsed.*

*This Article's "without cause" termination provision specifies the "unwinding" provisions of the Treaty. Any underwriting profit or loss sustained by those policies issued before termination will remain the property and responsibility of the parties under the terms of this Agreement as if no termination had occurred. Only when those policies have all been terminated and all required payments rendered, can both of the contracting parties be considered to have fulfilled their obligations to one another.*

*Under termination "with cause" (DWL's option), the Producer and InsCo forfeit all rights to future underwriting gains. However, this also shelters InsCo from any future underwriting losses. This Article provides a financial deterrent to discourage the Producer from moving his business to another carrier before the initial thirty-six-month period has elapsed.*

REINSURANCE PORTION - ARTICLE X

Errors and Omissions. It is understood and agreed that inadvertent errors or omissions concerning the business ceded under this contract shall not diminish nor invalidate the liabilities of InsCo, Producer or DWL hereunder.

*The last Article defines the conditions and remedies for any inadvertent errors or omissions in the cession of business under the treaty. If DWL inadvertently makes an error, and it can reasonably be shown to be inadvertent, InsCo will remain liable under the terms of the Agreement after rectification of the error, as if no error had occurred. This protects the integrity of the Agreement even if a clerical error occurs.*

IN WITNESS WHEREOF, the parties hereto have caused this instrument to be duly executed on this _______ day of _________________________, 199_____

ATTEST: DWL

_________________________ by______________________________

ATTEST: Producer

_________________________ by______________________________

*Execution by DWL and the Producer are the final items to consider. These signatures should be attested to by someone familiar with the persons executing the Agreement.*

Having been appointed by Producer to assume certain risks of DWL under the terms and conditions of the Reinsurance portion of this Agreement, this company does hereby agree to all the terms and conditions herein and has caused this instrument to be duly executed on this ______ day of ________________________, 199____

ATTEST: InsCo

____________________ by____________________________

*The final signature to this treaty is an officer of the insurance company (InsCo) designated by the Producer to assume the credit insurance risks from DWL. It is a good idea to have the Producer attest to the signature of the person executing this Agreement for InsCo to assure DWL that the appointment of the company (InsCo) was indeed made by the Producer. If the Producer attests to the signature, it will be very difficult to ever allege that DWL ceded underwriting profit to a reinsurer that was not appointed by the Producer.*

# Index

# ACKNOWLEDGEMENTS

During the long process of producing this book, we have received tremendous support from our industry, our staff, and our spouses. In the writing of the text we received technical assistance and review from Steve Burke, Walter Duer, Jim Gordon, Tom Haney, Greg Hixon, Larry Main, and Don Taylor.

Once the text was drafted a number of industry people took time from their busy schedules to review the drafts. Their comments honed the material and added a great deal to its usefulness and its readability. For this we wish to thank Chris Barbour, Mike Boyd, Kyle Campbell, Lloyd Gearhart, Arden Hetland, Mike Humphries, Jeff Lukash, Julie Messing, Paul Schreiber, Larry Scharfstein, and John Tiller.

Susan Aldinger, Brian Ulery, and Angela Hammerly of CreditRe Corporation, and Eleanor Chumley, Terry Donegan, Rachel Byers, Rick March, Bill Settles, and Ron Mailho of the Mailho Network participated in the development and production of the book. We think you will find the text readable and attractively laid out. Much of the credit for this goes to Becky Rohrer for a superb job of desktop publishing and Nancy Prine's usual fine job of editing and proofreading.

Terrie Mailho and Connie Fagg are integral to our personal and business life. Both play critical roles in operating our corporations on a day-to-day basis and maintaining a sense of permanence and stability in a world that involves over 100,000 miles a year of travel for each of us.

Steve would like to give grateful thanks to his dad for the shining example of stability, integrity, and honesty. Dad has always been there when needed. Special thanks goes to Steve's mother for encouraging him to strive beyond limits imposed by others. Together, his parents have been the solid platform resulting in his decade-long successful entrepreneurship. Gary would like to express his thanks to his mother and brother for their support through the years.

We believe strongly in the credit insurance industry. It provides a much needed sense of security that has over 75 years of proven acceptance by consumers. The benefits the dealership receives from the sale of this product are well-deserved and an integral aspect of the industry that has done so much to enhance the consumer borrowing environment.

We hope the book adds to your knowledge of the business and that this knowledge adds to your bottom line. We welcome your comments or questions.

Gary Fagg
John S. Mailho
November 1, 1992

CREDITRE CORPORATION
4107 Greenway Court
Colleyville, TX 76034
Phone: (817) 788-8121
Fax: (817) 788-8123

Mailho Company
3650 White Alder
Sonoma, CA 95476
Phone: (800) 262-4546
Fax: (707) 996-6397

# ABOUT MAILHO COMPANY

Mailho Company was established in the late seventies to serve the insurance community. Consulting on various administrative aspects of credit insurance operations, the Company began to specialize in reinsurance marketing programs. It created and implemented state-of-the-art overseas-domiciled reinsurance concepts that continue to be used today.

The Company is a decentralized operation with seven offices throughout the United States; these are considered nodes of the Mailho Network. Each office has its own specialty, adding to the multidimensional services offered to client overseas reinsurance companies. The Company subscribes to a decentralization approach, having found that highly-talented people do not live in one nice, neat, convenient community, but are scattered throughout the United States. Thus, the Company has representation in such well-known communities as Circleville, Grapevine, Rouge River, Selma and Woodstock. The Mailho Company went to the talent, rather than try to uproot and attract these highly-skilled professionals to an unfamiliar city.

As this book goes to press, Mailho Company has handled the formation of over fourteen hundred and fifty (1,450+) reinsurance companies for automobile dealers. Reinsurers were formed to allow dealers to participate in the underwriting profits of aftermarket insurance business from dealerships located in every state of the United States. The Mailho Company has begun its planned expansion to serve dealers in the North American Free Trade Zone, the European Community, and the explosive South American market. The Company will export state of the art aftermarket compensation concepts to dealerships throughout the World.

The corporate philosophy, borrowed from a successful Minnesota automobile dealer chain, is that the customer is first, employees second, and profits are third. At no time will these priorities be changed. This concept has served the Mailho Company well and will remain the foundation of its continuing operations in the United States and expanding markets in the remainder of the World.

# ABOUT CREDITRE CORPORATION

CREDITRE provides high-quality training material and programs about loan-related insurance products; and management, actuarial, and accounting consulting services to insurers and reinsurers underwriting these insurance products.

Our goal is to provide services that enhance the availability of loan-related insurance products. The central focus is on credit life and disability insurance. Natural auxiliary areas are loan-related property and casualty products and service contracts.

The corporation provides specialized consulting services to credit insurers, producer-owned reinsurers, financial institutions, and automobile dealerships. Our professional staff has extensive knowledge in all aspects of loan-related products and is prepared to provide complete services in these product areas. We have a strong commitment to training and teaching. Various seminars are offered to train home office personnel. In addition we will expand our list of publications to provide the industry with the written resources to expand the level of product knowledge.

In summary, we want to assist in raising the knowledge level of our entire industry to enhance the value to the insureds, increase profitability to insurers, and increase fee income to the producers of the business.

# ORDER FORM

Name________________________________________

Company______________________________________

Address______________________________________

City_________________________________________

State______________________ Zip______________

Phone________________________________________

PRICES:

A. Money on the Table:
   $40.00 per copy.

B. Credit Life and Disability Insurance:
   $40.00 per copy.

C. A Study Guide for Credit Life and Disability Insurance:
   $20.00 per copy.

D. An Introduction to Credit Life and Disability Insurance:
   $15.00 per copy; $10.00 each for 10 or more

| ORDER: | Price | No. | Total |
|---|---|---|---|
| A. | $40 | ___ | _____ |
| B. | $40 | ___ | _____ |
| C. | $20 | ___ | _____ |
| D. | $15/$10 | ___ | _____ |

Total amount of order: $__________

Make checks payable and send orders to:

CREDITRE CORPORATION
4201 Brown Trail, Ste 102
Colleyville, TX 76034

Allow 2 weeks for delivery. All books will be shipped 4th class book rate unless special handling is arranged. Inquiries may be directed to (817) 788-8121. Orders may also be faxed to (817) 788-8123. Prepaid orders are appreciated.